PRAISE

T0244056

Tabitha's words cut to the heart of our performance and perfectionism, stripping away the layers we've built up from years of being rejected. Through Scripture's truths, she empowers readers to follow Christ's example into forgiveness, not bitterness, into security, not scarcity, and into freedom rather than bondage. I recommend this book to any Christian desiring to trade the approval of people for the unchanging favor of God.

—PHYLICIA MASONHEIMER, founder and
CEO, Every Woman a Theologian

If you've ever felt the bitter sting of rejection, this book is meant to find you. With a full-bodied call to reacquaint ourselves with the God who sees us and walks with us, Tabitha steps into these pages as a light bearer and witness to the goodness of God. As you'll learn through this story unfolding, she isn't afraid to go first in sharing her scars and testimonies. Laced with beautiful breath prayers that serve as rest stops throughout, this book is a redemptive invitation to learn how to walk differently through the pain with resilience and faith to guide your path.

—HANNAH BRENCHER, author of
The Unplugged Hours and *Come Matter Here*

Rejection stings, especially to a weary soul—but God's love is the healing balm to restoring even the most painful things. That truth is so beautifully woven into Tabitha's book, *Loyal in His Love*. It's poetic, dreamy, and embedded with God's truth. What a gift to readers everywhere!

—TONI COLLIER, speaker, podcast host, and author of
Brave Enough to Be Broken and *Broken Crayons Still Color*

Have you ever felt abandoned by someone you should have been able to trust or profoundly hurt and disillusioned by the church? If so, you are not alone. Through personal narrative, honest reflection, psychological insight, and gospel hope, Tabitha Panariso reminds us amid our fears and threatening cynicism that "God is not only *with* us. But God is *for* us!" Unlike people and institutions that fail and falter, Christ is faithful, calling us *beloved* and welcoming us to practice resurrection, not by denying the hard stuff, but by discovering the depth of his love and kindness.

—KELLY M. KAPIC, author of *You're Only Human*

This book is a love letter to every one of us who have ever felt abandoned or rejected, forgotten by a world that only seems to celebrate the shiny, shiny perfect people, the ones who have never known what it's like to have *hard* in their story. Tabitha's words—equal parts pain, poetry, and salve to still-open wounds—took me by the hand and reminded me that my worth and belonging were never up to other people. At a time when we've never felt lonelier, I can't think of a more desperately needed message. Honest, raw, compelling, and most of all, healing, *Loyal in His Love* is a *must*-read!

—MARY MARANTZ, bestselling author of *Dirt* and
Underestimated, host of *The Mary Marantz Show*

Loyal in His Love is a balm for the broken-hearted, a gentle hand extended to those crushed by rejection. Tabitha's words do more than soothe; they breathe life into the weary soul like a kindred friend. With a poet's grace and a therapist's precision, she invites us to see rejection not as a final blow but as a divine invitation to deeper intimacy with God. Within the pages, you'll find more than fleeting comfort—you'll find the steady pulse of Christ's love, a love that restores, revives, and reshapes our pain into a vessel of hope. This book is not just a healing remedy but a lifeline to the heart that needs to know that rejection does not define them—God's loyal pursuit does.

—CHARAIA RUSH, author of *Courageously Soft*

As followers of Christ, we often struggle with how to speak to the wounds and rejection that all of us face at one point or another. Tabitha serves as a tender guide, using the Word and her own experience to advise us on how to navigate these seasons honestly without being swallowed by bitterness. This is a much needed resource for the body of Christ.

—BRENNA BLAIN, contemporary theologian and author

This book is a master class in healing from rejection. It is equal parts page-turning memoir, profound theology, practical teaching, and timeless spiritual wisdom. Tabitha has mined the deepest depths of her story to unearth the truest truths, all of which she envelops with gentle, exhilarating hope. If you have experienced rejection in your life, this book will leave you feeling not only seen but also shepherded and restored.

—SHARON HODDE MILLER, author of *The Cost of Control: Why We Crave It, the Anxiety It Gives Us, and the Real Power God Promises*

Loyal in His Love is a compelling and grace-filled invitation to encounter the redemptive love of Jesus Christ in the midst of deep emotional wounds caused by rejection, abandonment, and betrayal. Tabitha Panariso masterfully weaves personal story and biblical truth, reminding us that God meets us in our brokenness and joyfully brings healing. This book offers hope and restoration to those who feel abandoned or rejected, guiding readers to experience the transformative healing power of the gospel in their lives.

—JUSTIN S. HOLCOMB, bishop, author, and seminary professor

Amid what the surgeon general has called "an epidemic of loneliness," *Loyal in His Love* stands as a salient reminder that a quality relationship with our maker is indeed more than a platitude. Panariso highlights the root of contemporary spiritual malaise in tandem with trauma experts who consider all trauma as occurring within the context of relationship. This work is timely, applicable, and one of the most hard-hitting commentaries on what the absence of quality connection to God's love has done to recent generations, while also offering a gentle reminder of and steps toward reclaiming our rightful connection to the Father.

—JOSHUA KREIMEYER, associate professor of counseling, Colorado Christian University

Loyal in His Love artfully unveils the essence of rejection, exploring its impact on our hearts and minds, while gently sowing seeds of belonging, hope, and healing. It guides readers toward Jesus, highlighting his experiences of rejection and demonstrating how he navigated these painful moments. Through its pages, readers find connection, validation, encouragement, and hope, offering solace to those who have faced rejection from friends, family, church, and even themselves.

—LIZ WIGGINS, assistant dean of the School of Counseling at Colorado Christian University

Tabitha Panariso poured her heart into *Loyal in His Love*, and it shows. In a world where the sting of rejection and abandonment is all too familiar, Tabitha's words are a soothing balm for the soul. Her writing is both poetic and piercing, rooted in biblical truth that points us to the reality of God's unwavering love. What stands out most is Tabitha's profound understanding of the human heart, which shines through in her heartfelt reflections. I savored every word written in this book, and I know it will be a trustworthy companion for many on their journeys to healing.

—CASSANDRA SPEER, bestselling author, Bible teacher, and vice president of Her True Worth

LOYAL
IN HIS
LOVE

LOYAL IN HIS LOVE

AN INVITATION TO BE HELD BY JESUS WHEN OTHERS LET YOU GO

TABITHA PANARISO

ZONDERVAN
REFLECTIVE

ZONDERVAN REFLECTIVE

Loyal in His Love
Copyright © 2025 by Tabitha Panariso

Published in Grand Rapids, Michigan, by Zondervan. Zondervan is a registered trademark of The Zondervan Corporation, L.L.C., a wholly owned subsidiary of HarperCollins Christian Publishing, Inc.

Requests for information should be addressed to customercare@harpercollins.com.

Zondervan titles may be purchased in bulk for educational, business, fundraising, or sales promotional use. For information, please email SpecialMarkets@Zondervan.com.

Library of Congress Cataloging-in-Publication Data

Names: Panariso, Tabitha, 1986- author.
Title: Loyal in His love : an invitation to be held by Jesus when others let you go / Tabitha Panariso.
Description: Grand Rapids, Michigan : Zondervan Reflective, [2024]
Identifiers: LCCN 2024026142 (print) I LCCN 2024026143 (ebook) I ISBN 9780310160205 (softcover) I ISBN 9780310160212 (ebook) I ISBN 9780310160229 (audio)
Subjects: LCSH: Love--Religious aspects--Christianity. I Rejection (Psychology)-- Religious aspects--Christianity. I BISAC: RELIGION / Christian Living / Personal Growth I PSYCHOLOGY / Psychopathology / Post-Traumatic Stress Disorder (PTSD)
Classification: LCC BV4639 .P3114 2024 (print) I LCC BV4639 (ebook) I DDC 231/.6--dc23/eng/20240812
LC record available at https://lccn.loc.gov/2024026142
LC ebook record available at https://lccn.loc.gov/2024026143

Published in association with The Bindery Agency, www.TheBinderyAgency.com.

Cover design: Faceout Studio, Jeff Miller
Cover art: Shutterstock
Interior design: Sara Colley

Printed in the United States of America

24 25 26 27 28 LBC 5 4 3 2 1

To Ethan,
my unwavering source of strength and love,
you've held me through it all

CONTENTS

FOREWORD

Have you ever held a handful of seeds?

Maybe you've planted gardens, plucked dahlias tended by your own hands, sunk your teeth into a red tomato sliced and salted and dripping down the corners of your mouth, said a prayer for hail to miss your peppers, looked at the sky and doubted that this summer would bring enough rain. Or maybe you've just dreamed a garden, standing at a farmer's market stall, wondering when your life would not be too small. Too small to own a home or have a yard or hold more than screaming babies or pillboxes full of treatments you wish you didn't need. Small.

Small like the seeds that start the life that bears good things.

Don't worry. This is not a book about gardening. You didn't misread the title. But it is a book that follows the same life cycle as seeds. It is a book about growing a life blooming with more than weeds.

I want that life, and I imagine you do too.

My pal Tabitha Panariso is more than a skilled therapist and fantastic friend. She is a woman who has let her grief become a garden.

When Jesus told his friends about his coming death, he likened it to a seed. "I speak from my heart," he told them. "If a seed is unplanted, it remains only one seed, but if it dies, falls to the earth, and enters the ground, it will then grow and become many seeds" (John 12:23, First Nations Version). I don't fancy the feeling of falling. I don't enjoy sitting in the dark. I don't want to watch my center split open. I don't like to sense my core exposed.

But this is the only way a seed becomes something stunning. In botany, there is a term called *scarification*. Many large seeds or seeds with thick, hard exteriors must be split open in order to grow. The gardener must scar the seed—by fire, by knife, by sulfur—for the seed to open the cells within it to oxygen and water and light.

Sometimes we must be split open to grow. We must be wounded and buried before we become the fullest, most fragrant versions of ourselves.

Several years ago, when I was first getting to know Tabitha, she shared that she was going to delete all of her social media accounts. For a writer, especially for a writer with dreams of becoming an author, *this* was bold. Typically, a writer must gather a following of many thousands of readers before any publisher will take them seriously enough to risk the investment of publishing. And Tabitha was on her way there. On the outside, it looked like Tabitha was burying her dream. It was the opposite of conventional wisdom, and the wisest thing I've ever seen a hopeful-author choose.

Tabitha was nicking the seed of her own dream because she sensed she needed to learn how to live buried—to learn how to trust that life happens in the dark before it rises to the light. She discerned that she needed to spend time hidden, nurturing life in ways only she and her family could see, before trying to grow anything beautiful for others. The day Tabitha deleted her accounts was the day I decided she will always be someone with wisdom I want to hear.

And now, years of friendship later, I know that she did it because she was letting the woundings in her life become like the scar to the seed—the start of something stunning for more than herself. The book you are holding in your hands is the bouquet of flowers Tabitha let grow from the scars in her story. I'll let her tell you those stories herself, but for now, I hope you'll hold out your hand and imagine that the most painful pieces of *your* story might just be the start of something stunning too.

—K.J. RAMSEY, licensed therapist, author of
This Too Shall Last, *The Lord Is My Courage*,
and *The Book of Common Courage*

INTRODUCTION

F or most of my life, I didn't have any pictures of myself as a baby.

When I was only five years old, sometime after my mom divorced my biological father, he discarded whatever memories we had. I would never see those photos again—like I'd never see him again.

I had been abandoned.

Like any other little girl might, I felt my dad's absence acutely. But more troubling than what he took away was what he left behind: unseen wounds. His absence marked me. And while it would be years before I understood the extent of the damage his leaving would do, I learned quickly that when someone you love turns their back on you, it can forever shape everything you believe. Our past inevitably informs our present. And if we let it, the past can shape our future too.

The wounds that went unnoticed during my childhood refused to stay hidden in adulthood. It was unavoidable. The ache of rejection lurked behind every relationship and opportunity. Sometimes it would hit me when I least expected it: Friends who didn't choose me. A church that chose to forget me. There were times, even, when I would betray myself.

Often I wondered, *Have others experienced such rejection or felt it as deeply?*

For a long time, I thought I was isolated in this pain. But rejection is far more common than I realized. It's safe to say, everyone experiences it. Yet we're forced to pretend we're not impacted by it. So we don't talk about it. We minimize it.

"Everything happens for a reason!" we might exclaim, every word spoken with a gulp of air and a smile plastered on our face.

We bury our anger and anguish in an unmarked grave. We try to forget. But the mound of disappointment only grows. We can't deny the way it takes up space and the way it feels like it might consume us. We can't avoid the way it exposes us. Our very identity is put on trial simply by its ongoing, looming presence.

In this way, rejection almost always feels like certain death. It's no wonder we sometimes crumble under the weight of its aftermath or in anticipation of our encounter with it. We worry about what might be left once we've pulled the remnants from rejection's ruins.

Nothing goes untouched.

Whether we like it or not, rejection changes us. Its roots dig deep, jeopardizing any possibility of natural growth or, often, healthy and sustainable relationships. It attempts to build barriers between God and us—preventing us from connecting with God in the way God originally designed.

While it's unlikely that you have experienced rejection

exactly as I have, we both know its pain, its seemingly indelible impact, and the debris it leaves behind.

We strive desperately to be accepted, or we hide in fear of being seen and then discounted. Cynicism and mistrust corrode our relationships. It becomes harder to believe we belong or are loved no matter how many times someone tells us. We make ourselves quieter and smaller. We discount our value for the sake of others' comfort.

These strategies to save ourselves only betray us. They can't sustain us.

These are the bandages that scarcely cover the hemorrhaging of a lost relationship or dream.

To be clear, I'm not disinclined to believe God forges new paths for us when others don't work out. When a door closes, God could crack a window. But who am I when I crawl through it? Rejection can compel us to change course and redirect us, but it won't heal us. While I fully believe that God is sovereign, he isn't to blame for other people's choices. We don't always have a compelling meaning to latch onto when life doesn't work out the way we want it to. When we've been left behind, we may never know why. We may never see our broken relationships repaired. Some dreams won't come true, and we're challenged to make room for something different and new.

There has to be more than platitudes to ease our pain.

There has to be more we can do than run and hide.

If you're holding this book, I assume you believe and hope for that too.

$$\backsim$$

In 2022, I flew to Texas to celebrate my grandma's ninetieth birthday. It had been twenty-five years since I'd last visited her home. Since then, I'd come to realize the importance of story, and I hoped I might find a few glimpses of my own. While there, I endured the humidity, watched my grandmother single-handedly scare off a copperhead snake, and, on the last night, found a part of myself that had been missing.

I sat in my grandma's dimly lit living room where endless photo albums were collecting dust. One by one, I sifted through years of history and family legacy. Hours went by. Finally, I turned a page to see a picture of me as a newborn, wrapped in a yellow swaddling blanket. And then another photo of me cradled in my mom's arms on Christmas Day.

My father's presence was reflected in the massive bottle of liquor that sat under the Christmas tree beside my mom— his addiction a part of our lives even then.

Finding these photos was a gift; a catalyst for fully realizing that I had been held even when I had been forgotten. In that moment, in the dark of night, I knew to whom I had always belonged.

Though I had searched my entire life to be welcomed and seen, it hadn't come the way I thought it would. It hadn't yet come through other people. Instead, it came through the Lord.

At the risk of sounding hopelessly discouraging, people often disappoint us. They leave. They ignore. They forget. And we do this too. We are human after all. But despite all this, we get a choice. We get to choose whether to die by their rejection or to live in and through Christ instead.

Rejection doesn't have to be the truest thing about you.

How?

How do we even begin to heal this wound when we don't have others in our lives whom we feel safe turning to? How can we move through abandonment—betrayal even—without losing parts of ourselves in the process?

I've spent my whole life trying to answer this question.

And the answer didn't come easy.

More than anything, I value honesty. So what I want to tell you is that what we're going to do together in these pages might be difficult. I am acutely aware of the depths our hearts must plumb when journeying through our stories. It requires not just an awareness of the parts of ourselves that resist healing, but also a willingness to hold them in our hands ever so gently and give them over to Jesus.

Resistance is a part of the process; in fact, it reveals the fragments of our hearts that are the most lost—razor sharp and ready to cut. Resistance is a truth-teller. With it, discomfort and uncertainty are welcome too. It's not simple to rewrite or even more clearly see the story you've been living in for all this time. And so you have permission to tread lightly. When you happen to feel any of those responses rise within you—when you get that visceral reaction to slam this book shut and deny what's inside of you—stay curious. Take notice of it. Sit with it.

What is your heart trying to tell you?

Just as I hope these words might hold space for you—in the hazy place of self-discovery and God revelation—I hope you might do the same for yourself.

I wouldn't really consider this a self-help book. Not in the usual sense, anyway.

Rather, it is a process of becoming. It is an opportunity to embody the way and the truth and the life that are of Jesus and let them change us—from the inside out. It is an invitation to resurrection, for what feels like death to us and what *was* death to Christ offers us a new way of living life.

It is a love letter. For you and for me.

It is a witness to what so many of us fear to speak of but what often haunts us.

It is the atlas of my heart—and the mountains and valleys that I have had to trek as someone who has been rejected, abandoned, and betrayed.

It is an integration of all the pieces of ourselves—our psychology, our theology, and our spirituality—in order that we can reclaim them and that they might heal together as one.

And I am your hopeful guide. I'm walking alongside you through the narrows of our shared pain, shining a beam of light into every unseen place so that the shards of your heart that have been obscured can be brought into the light.

It is time to come out of hiding.

I can't promise that you won't experience rejection again. You most likely will. However, what I can promise is that you *will* find strength in surrender and freedom in living openhandedly. Because when we put our lives in the right and righteous hands of Christ, we'll find that this thing that wants to keep us nailed to the ground can't keep us down forever. We won't let rejection continue to serve us up a litany of endings and regret.

Rejection often feels like death. But I'm not here to tell you it's less than death—it's *more* than it.

We only need to gaze at the broken and bloody body of Christ brutally affixed to the cross to discover that rejection is a promise. The blood that dripped from Jesus's crown of thorns declared an outcome that the crowds of people who cried, "Crucify him!" couldn't yet see.

Jesus knew firsthand what it was like to be rejected. We see it in his death. And yet he is remembered for his life and his coming back to it.

He's proof that we can be too.

He is proof of the loyal love of God. He shepherds us into God's hands and hems us in with hope.

Hope embraces the forsaken. It meets us in the ditches where we've been left and neglected, strewn about like discarded trash. Christ descends from his throne to tend to us. He calls us beloved and blessed.

To be beloved is one thing, but to live like it is quite another.

Though rejection can place a heavy burden on us, we are free to unpack the weight of that pain, laying it down brick by brick. But instead of walls, we'll build bridges.

From hurt to healing.

From brokenness to wholeness.

From loneliness to belonging.

From forsakenness to belovedness.

All the way back to Christ, to others, and to ourselves.

Rejection isn't our enemy, but our companion— impatiently waiting to be both redeemed and restored.

Together, we will travel from death to life.

For us, rejection isn't the end. It's only the beginning.

A NOTE ON BREATH PRAYERS

Breath prayers offer a simple yet effective means of spiritual formation by combining deep breathing with the truth of God's Word. With each inhale and exhale, you bring both your body and mind in alignment with the Lord.

Breathwork has numerous benefits. It calms our mind, alleviates our pain, and restores our nervous system. As such, it supports clarity of thought and focus.

Breath prayers allow us to "pray continually"—anywhere and at any time. You can say them either out loud or silently. But as you do, be sure to breathe deeply and slowly.

At the beginning of each chapter, you'll find a breath prayer that complements it. Each one serves as a point of reference and a means of introspection—something to return to time and time again.

May you find peace in each interlude, and power to persevere with each pause.

PART ONE

FROM DEATH . . .

INHALE

I am in need.
You listen intently.

EXHALE

I call on you.
You deliver me.

BASED ON PSALM 116

CHAPTER 1

INEVITABLE DEMISE

I sat hunched on the floor of my bedroom with my knees cradled in my arms and the phone teetering on my shoulder as it pressed hard against my ear. It served as an anchor, keeping me steady as the floor fell out from under me.

On the other end of the line was my biological father. We hadn't spoken for at least a decade.

He disappeared when I was five. Without a word. Without a trace. He drifted away and out of my life as quickly as any of the memories I had of him.

I felt tender, open to the possibility of what I could only describe as finally being found. Like most kids my age, I didn't yet know myself. I was still in the midst of maturing. I was searching for where I belonged and to whom. None of the answers I'd been given felt right. None of them felt like who I believed—or wanted—myself to be.

Perhaps, I thought, this man—my *dad*—was the missing piece.

My mom's anxious pacing right outside my bedroom matched the frantic beating of my heart.

Still, I couldn't help but swell with hope. It was as if some part of me had been uncorked. Longing bubbled out from inside me. Maybe it all had been some sort of misunderstanding. Maybe he wanted me in his life after all. Maybe I could keep this massive, empty hole that had made its home within me from eating me alive.

He was the only ghost to ever haunt me.

Was he real?

I didn't know.

I wanted to. I wanted to know him.

So when my mom gave me a choice to talk with him, I eagerly grabbed at the phone.

We can't help but ache to restore that which has been broken.

"Hello," I said into the phone. "It's me."

Your daughter.

Your flesh and blood.

And then he spoke.

Though I had never had a sip of alcohol, it was clear to me that he was inebriated. Drunk—with regret or liquid courage, I'm not sure which. But only barely present all the same. He would ask me a question, and then again, and then once more, never sure where the conversation had left off. I tried to navigate his fuzziness with my own clear headedness. I wanted so desperately to form some sort of connection between us. But that didn't last long. I could feel myself begin to drown from the surge of tears gathering in my eyes. As he blathered on incoherently, I cut him off and told him I had to go as I ran to my mom to give her the phone.

I couldn't have known just how wounded I was. I couldn't have known how his absence would impact me—not just then, but to this day. Yet at that moment I concluded that something had to be wrong with me. Surely I was broken if I couldn't make my own father love me.

It was easy to believe. No one ever thought to tell me differently.

I was the problem. So I'd have to change.

I dive-bombed back onto the floor of my bedroom, swept up in the grief of a life I'd never know. I had been abandoned once again by my parent—someone who was supposed to have chosen me. So I made a choice. I'd never let anyone see that part of me again—that heart that gaped wide open with trust and hope. In the aftermath of being left, I would begin to abandon myself and others too.

I had to bury the pain, and with it, the questions—the ones that were too hard to answer:

What did I have to do to be loved?

Would I ever be enough to be wanted?

In the years that followed, I began to believe the story that I was easy to leave. Every relationship became transactional. If I gave, performed, and conformed, then I could receive. I held most people at a distance—only letting them see what I wanted them to see.

I carried this burden willingly. I exchanged one death for another.

I didn't have to be me if it meant I could belong to others.

As humans, this is precisely how we survive—through our belonging. Our survival hinges on the acceptance of our families and the groups in which we exist. It's not just an emotional necessity; it's visceral. To be rejected is to be denied a need.

This is why it hurts so much when others turn their backs on us. It signals what feels like our inevitable demise. Rejection feels like death. Abandonment devastates the soul. Betrayal feels like a never-ending affliction. What we experience after someone we love moves on without us or we lose out on something we hoped for is more than just a lesson to be learned. Our brain cannot tell the difference between a broken arm and our broken heart. It often cannot tell the difference between rejections that matter and those that don't. They provoke the same pain. Each one travels the same path to tell us we're not safe, to spring us into action, to spur us to self-protect.[1]

Where love quickens our heart, denial slows it—quite literally.[2] Rejection muffles the organ that pumps life through us, helping us move and breathe and live and play.

We can see the impact of rejection in our physical bodies, knowing it mirrors what is also occurring within us spiritually. In this case, the heart that suffers rejection can't be cured. It must be resuscitated. Its condition warrants more than just platitudes; it merits the full attention of a loyal and loving God. It deserves our care and our acknowledgment.

In my own life, I have seen how rejection has taken hold of my senses. It dug its fingers into my flesh and held me back from fully experiencing life the way I wished I could. Often it blinded me to a love that invited me in.

I looked to perfectionism to save me. If I could be who I was expected to be, then I could avoid the pain of rejection and failure. It wasn't fear that motivated me; it was self-protection. Insecurity abounded as I doubted who I was and whether I was good enough. Rejection twisted itself into the fabric of my DNA, making it hard to divorce myself from it. I clamored to fill myself with what I thought might satisfy—anything that made me feel loved: an accomplishment, an award, or living a life that looked the way the world thought it should.

Rejection is inevitable. We've all experienced it in one way or another. Each experience ranges in both depth and width, as well as impact.

Maybe, as with me, one of your parents left you. Or maybe they just neglected you, time and time again not seeing and knowing you as you longed to be.

Or perhaps your spouse, the one you committed your whole life to, betrayed you. They put themselves in the arms and the heart of another.

It could be that you simply feel othered, unable to make a friend or form a community—hard-pressed to connect.

Maybe you have been ostracized from a group you once called family.

You might find that friendships have dissolved, unable to withstand the passing of time, season, or misunderstanding. Those friends might have blocked you from all parts of their lives. Where you once walked together, now you walk alone.

Maybe a family member refuses to engage with you. They've cut you off without a clear understanding of why. For some reason, they won't give you another opportunity to redeem yourself. You're left feeling helpless and hopeless.

Rejection is in the heartbreak you feel after a breakup, and especially when they say, but perhaps don't mean, "It's not you, it's me."

Or maybe you were simply turned down by someone you hoped to connect with more intimately, more deeply.

But rejection doesn't only show up in obvious expressions such as these.

We can feel it from a cold shoulder, an invisible wall placed between us and another, in unspoken gestures or inside jokes, hurtful words or unextended invites.

Rejection looks like being blocked without warning, maliciously talked about by others, or even ghosted: One day everything is fine, and then the next . . . it's not.

Rejection is in the deafening silence that happens when you walk away and no one comes after you. It's when no one stands up for you when your reputation is being tarnished.

It looks like the injustice of being treated differently because of prejudice or racism.

Though rejection persists in the interactions we have with others, it's also part of the risks we take in forming our lives, such as interviewing for that job or opportunity we want, holding our breath for the phone call we hope is coming and then hearing, "We regret to inform you . . ."

". . . you didn't get the job."

". . . we won't accept this proposal."

". . . we've gone in another direction."

Rejection is more than what happens to us. It is how it makes us feel.

Betrayed. Estranged. Abandoned.

Dismissed. Forsaken. Spurned.

All these forms of rejection cause us to experience a range of anger, anxiety, sadness, shame, guilt, loneliness, confusion, unworthiness, and embarrassment. How has it made you feel?

Without a doubt, it hurts. It makes us feel small. It makes us feel less than.

For many of us, rejection ravages the soul as we smile wide on the outside, pretending that all is well.

On the inside, rejection of all kinds is distressing. It activates a physiological response embedded in us from the very beginning of time, when our communities were tribes and not sprawling, industrial cities. We knew that to be disconnected from others meant certain death. If we were banished from the group—before we had air conditioning and vending machines—we could be certain our literal demise was imminent. We'd have to protect ourselves. And the odds were not in our favor. Thus, we'd do anything to avoid exile. Our lives depended on being seen and not forgotten. It's not good for us to be alone (Gen. 2:18).

Our bodies know this to be true, even if our minds don't always. When we're threatened with isolation, it's only natural that we'd feel ourselves moving into a stress response— that we'd physically feel despair and even desperation.

But in modern society, we've tried to rewrite and minimize our need for connection. Self-sufficiency reigns like a king in checkmate, standing in place, unable to move.

These days, though we're not forced to forage for food and shelter, rejection still significantly influences our social, emotional, and physical well-being. It lowers self-esteem. It causes us to question ourselves. And it can also hijack our physical well-being, weakening our immune systems.

In some people, rejection can lead to aggression, even violent bursts of behavior in retribution against those who hurt them.

We tell ourselves rejection is merely redirection—that perhaps God is simply protecting us from a future we can't quite envision. That all sounds fine. At least it feels like something we can hold on to.

Yet bandages can't fix broken hearts. Platitudes do more than placate us; they numb us. We are not weak or less holy when we want more. We are wired for wholeness. We were made for each other. And God wants to repair what has been fractured. God wants us to live in the freedom of being loved, not in fear of being forsaken.

When our youngest son entered kindergarten, he was thrilled to go to school with his brother and sister. He was also hesitant to leave me. To him, each day was long and never-ending. Multiple times throughout the beginning of the year, I would remind him that though he couldn't see me, he could trust that I loved him and I would be there at the end of the day to take him home.

I would arrive early to pick up the kids to avoid the cluster of chaos that would overwhelm the building each afternoon. It would always give me enough time to stand outside with the other parents to watch the kindergartners stream out the front doors. Most of them would emerge unsmiling, searching. I could see them scanning the crowd for their person, wanting to know if they had been remembered. Wanting to know, in their mind at least, if they were loved.

Then I would see him: Levi dutifully following his teacher, the same grimace stretching the sides of his face. His eyes would find mine. In seconds, he would transform. His apathy replaced with joy, he would brighten up like a bulb, the energy traveling through his body, almost electrifying him. He would move quickly to his teacher, bidding farewell with pep, and then turn to sprint, headlong, into my arms.

This is what it looks like to know you belong to someone who loves you.

It changes us. It brings us back to life.

When I imagine a life unburdened by rejection, I see my son.

And I think of all he has been given to allow him to live this way.

One of the foundational aspects of therapy is attachment theory. Based on the groundbreaking work of psychologists John Bowlby and Mary Ainsworth, attachment theory strongly suggests that the bonds we develop as children with our caregivers significantly impact both our well-being and the way that we form relationships as adults. It primarily has to do with connection, which establishes our sense of safety and security. When we've grown up securely attached, with our physical and emotional needs tended to, we're more likely to become confident, trusting, hopeful people. We're more likely to dive headlong into the rhythms of life—like my son.

At first glance, it might disappoint you to learn that our relationships with our primary caregivers make such an impact on us. We don't choose our family. We don't choose how we were raised or how we were or weren't cared for. We cannot change the past. However, we do get to choose how we want to move forward. What is empty can be filled. What seems broken, repaired. And what feels unseen and invisible, brought into the open.

We carry this longing deep in our hearts. We all want someone, anyone, to be looking for *us*. To show up for *us*. To love *us* as we are. Our longings are pleas and petitions— often asking us to do the work to alleviate what aches. These longings aren't something we can afford to ignore.

Working from Bowlby and Ainsworth's research, child psychologist Dan Siegel formed a powerful process one could use in supporting their children to form what we call a secure attachment. I believe these are the things that would help protect a heart from the pain of rejection and even the affliction of abandonment and betrayal. They are important to us because in establishing them in ourselves—and even feeling them in our bodies—we can begin to heal. It comes down to this. In order to feel secure, we must be:

SAFE. We do not feel afraid. We are in a secure and stable environment, both physically and emotionally. We know who we can rely on.
SEEN. We feel known. We know that someone is attuned to our needs, emotions, and experiences.

SOOTHED. We feel comforted. When we're in distress, we find support in regulating our emotions. We're able to be calmed.[3]

When these factors are in place, we can cultivate healthier relationships with others and even ourselves. We're more likely to feel confident—even indomitable. We can regulate our emotions and cope with stress. We may even find that we develop a greater sense of self-esteem. Risks don't feel as daunting.

While Siegel primarily focuses on applying these principles to the parent-child relationship, it can be argued that adults would also benefit from incorporating them into their lives.

Dan Siegel likens the process to showing up, which couldn't be more appropriate.

While we cannot force others to show up for us as adults, we can learn to show up for ourselves. It's not too late. We can develop practices that help us soothe and see ourselves. We can feel safe. Personally, I know how difficult this can be to do on our own. Thankfully, we don't have to. We can build a healthy relationship with ourselves by building one with Jesus—and in turn experience how that impacts all our other relationships and our lives for the better.

Maybe you've become accustomed to being forgotten. Maybe no one has really shown up for you in a long time. You are not alone. Jesus is coming for you.

In the New Testament, we meet a man who could do nothing for himself but wait (John 5).

We don't know much about him, save that he was an invalid who had made a home near the Pool of Bethesda in Jerusalem, which was known—perhaps ironically—as a house of mercy. It was a place for the blind, the lame, and the paralyzed—the outcast and forgotten. It must have been quite bleak, with every square foot covered by the bodies of those seemingly beyond repair.

They believed that every so often, an angel would come and stir the waters with its wing. If they could just muster enough strength to become the first to dip themselves into the pool, they would be healed of their afflictions.

This man had come to find relief, but instead remained to live in his brokenness. He lived at only the edge of mercy, it seemed, instead of plunging himself into its cold, forgiving water. He simply couldn't. It must have been a torturous existence. Time passed him by. Life unraveling.

No one showed up for him. Until Jesus did.

Jesus makes his way through this multitude of people, beelining toward this man's side. Jesus knows this man has been there for some time. And he shows up for him.

I don't know how long you've waited, but I know the doubt that can accompany us when it's been too long since someone came for us. We can convince ourselves that it's too late for us. We can believe that we are too stuck and unable to move. We can despair in our loneliness.

Then Jesus makes his way toward you in a crowded room.

He locks eyes with you.

What could this mean?

It's never too late to experience an encounter with Christ.

Jesus gets straight to the point.

Without hesitation or even introduction, Jesus asks this man a question: "Do you want to get well?" (John 5:6). It's an intimate question, one that isn't easily answered. Because it has less to do with our will and more to do with the posture of our heart. It beseeches us to surrender to the truth.

Can Jesus heal even *this* part of us? Can we give him all of *this* too?

Christ is asking,

"Can you see the parts of yourself that require my care?"

"Do you know that you are aching?"

"Are you willing to admit that you are weak and in need?"

Christ desires to hold the space for us that we don't always know how to, and often can't, hold for ourselves.

"Can't you see that the thing you thought would care for you, can't?"

We build our own pools of mercy. We dig our hands into the ground constructing superstitious beliefs around our behavior and our arduous wait—these are our attempts at coping with the hardship of rejection. We stay focused on stories that we don't even know to be true.

Though I can't be sure of your answer, know this: even the invalid couldn't speak it.

Even still, Jesus extended compassion and chose to support him. In that moment, he didn't indict him; he accepted him as he was. He doesn't wait for us to know the true power of who he is before inviting us to walk anew.

While the man at the pool couldn't respond to Jesus honestly, we can.

When we learn to say out loud what has happened to us, it begins to lose its hold on us.

First, it demonstrates that we can clearly see brokenness. It's real. Our eyes open to the ruins rejection has left in our hearts and our lives. We can begin somewhere. With Christ, we can pick up the pieces and put them back together again.

Second, when we name our pain, it demonstrates that we are bigger than it. We can interact with it. We can ease it. We can do something about it. It's no longer an unmovable wall, but rather an open door through which we can walk.

When we name our pain, we can separate ourselves from it. We have a tendency to personify our feelings. Instead of "I feel rejected," we claim, "I am rejected." We say, "I am lonely," instead of, "I feel lonely." These emotions begin to take on a life of their own. They often blind us. We can only see what hinders us. And it becomes us.

Let's take a step back. For just a moment, let's spread our emotions out before us and name them.

Stop for a moment. Close your eyes and visualize the wounds that have come from your experience with rejection, abandonment, or even betrayal. Lay each feeling that rises up within you all out before you. Imagine that you are sitting on a bench looking out into a street and that each of these emotions are passing by. There may be some that are quick to move away from you, and others that linger. Perhaps you invite them to sit with you, just for a moment.

They don't have to stay for long. And they are *not* you. Instead, they are your guests. You can extend them your helping hand, and provide them with the grace, mercy, and compassion that Christ gives to you.

I wonder if you've allowed yourself to sit with the ache of rejection and to name it.

Perhaps it's time. Maybe these margins can be a safe place to write down the story that's ever present in your mind—the moment you felt yourself shutting down because of the disappointment you experienced. You could let yourself speak aloud what you've held hostage for too long—in prayer or over coffee with a trusted friend.

Maybe you are more than aware of the ways rejection has hindered you and taken you captive. You're ready to yield and let Jesus free you.

When we bring to light those things we let lurk in the dark, our world changes. We change.

Just as Christ moved toward the man at the pool, Christ moves toward us so that we can receive what he has to offer us. He embodies a secure attachment. His presence gives this man the power to do what at first was impossible.

Like my son, like me, like you, we all can be transformed by being seen and pursued. We can reclaim a life of wholeness when we know that there is someone who wants nothing but good for us.

Jesus knows that, like us, this man wanted a different life.

We can't live the lives we want from a grave, buried under the weight of rejection.

Nor can we live our lives at the edge of waiting any longer.

"Then Jesus said to him, 'Get up! Pick up your mat and walk.' At once the man was cured; he picked up his mat and walked" (John 5:8–9).

What might it be like to walk after we've stumbled over the certainty of rejection?

We read that the man at the pool, at first, had no idea who had healed him. He was ignorant of Jesus's identity and power. But we aren't.

We know what to expect from Jesus—we know that no matter how deep our pain goes or how encumbered we are from suffering, Jesus will find and attend to us.

I want a life where I can move freely among others and with them too. I want a life that isn't marred by wounds. I don't want to be blinded by fear but made wide open by love. I don't want to have to second-guess myself or feel unsteady because I'm not sure where I belong. I want my life to be moored in the certainty that I am held—not by others or by myself but by the everlasting God who is unruffled by my weakness, unafraid of my questions or uncertainty, always reassuring, always holding my hand though it all and tending to every part of me.

I don't want to feel like I have to hold back or withdraw but that I can be fully myself, knowing I'm loved. I want to live fully alive. I want to give generously without expectation. I want relationships with others that aren't tainted by my frustrations. I want to see Jesus clearly in myself, in my life, and in others. I want that bottomless pit of desire for affirmation and validation to be filled.

I can't do this on my own. I've tried.

And like the man at Bethesda, in so many ways I have

looked to other people for help and been disappointed. They fail, even when they try. Truth is, they will only continue to do so. I have sat and waited for something, anything, to help me find a path away from the pain of rejection. But others can't fill what only fits God's unending love.

I didn't know I'd been blinded by contempt and debilitated by others' disapproval. I got a regular dopamine hit from validation. I was addicted to affirmation, acknowledgment, and achievement. Every dose was just enough to hide the bitterness growing inside me.

I was comfortable languishing in my brokenness. I dressed it up. It's easier to make it seem as if rejection hasn't hurt us—as if we're untouchable.

Until Christ comes along and asks, "Do you want to be healed?"

I don't want to live paralyzed anymore. I don't want rejection to get the final say in the way I live out the rest of my days. I don't want to live as a dead woman walking, unable to get close to others, to take risks, and to thrive.

Jesus. I want to be healed.

I am in need. I am hurting. Rejection has immobilized me.

Some of us may see the wreckage that has played out in our lives because of rejection, but we refuse to acknowledge the mess it has made in our hearts. Our denial is a detriment to our healing. It's not so much that Jesus needs to know— it's that he wants to know that we know.

Do you want to be healed?

I know the weariness of it all seeps deep into the sinews that connect muscle to bone, limiting our ability to get

19

up, to move. We don't have to know any more than this. We don't have to exercise any other strength than this: to name our need. At this moment, even if we're not yet sure of Jesus, even if God still feels distant or untrustworthy, Christ has moved toward us to invite us to pick up our mats and walk.

That's all that is required. Not a steady faith. Not certainty in what's to come. Instead, we get to hope that Christ could offer us something different and have courage to say what's difficult.

As with the man at Bethesda, our relationship to Christ isn't in question at this moment. The fact is, we may not be able to give much beyond our honesty. That's okay.

As we lay out our case before him, he listens to us. As we name our pain, he hears our pleas.

It is enough to know we are safe, that we are seen, and that Christ himself soothes our pain.

For even if we don't quite believe it yet, Christ will deliver our souls from death, our eyes from tears, and our feet from stumbling, and we will walk before the Lord in the land of the living (Ps. 116:8–9).

Let's stand and walk toward his goodness together.

Let's pick up what we've buried and walk forward with it. Let's claim it as part of our story and bear witness to what was—and what gets to be.

We are not meant to quiet the hungry parts of our soul or to fear to say out loud what we long to be restored. It does us no good to pretend when that is all that stands in the way of what we want most.

In exchange for our honesty, we receive healing.

In light of our need, Christ searches the dark. He comes for us.

Our groans to be seen will always be met with Christ's reply: I am with you. I am with you. I am with you.

INHALE

His banner over me
is love.

EXHALE

His name for me
is beloved.

BASED ON SONG OF SOLOMON 2:4 AND JOHN 15:9

CHAPTER 2

EVIDENCE OF THINGS NOT SEEN

As we lay side by side in our bed, my husband turned to me and asked, "Do you trust me?"

Ethan and I had been married for several years. We didn't know the hardship that lay ahead of us and we didn't know that the answer to this question would be needed to survive the days to come. But even in that moment, I felt as if it was welcoming an unburdening. It was the beginning of acknowledging a lie I'd held for far too long.

I could have held the truth close for the sake of what was expected of me. Instead I thought I'd try something a little less performative. Honesty.

I hesitated and then said, "I want to. But I don't know how."

Ethan is faithful and loyal. Without fail. But despite the evidence of who I knew him to be, there was something in me that questioned and doubted him. I realized in that moment, as I poured out my heart to my husband, that all this mistrust and insecurity wasn't a result of his failings; it was a burden I'd long carried from the failings of others. It was a result of my vision, of my perspective.

He met my eyes and said, "I understand." In the dark, for the first time I felt like I could finally see myself a little more clearly.

I could see that I had been blinded to the goodness that abounded not just in my marriage but in my friendships and elsewhere too. I had learned how to collect a body of evidence that was entirely circumstantial, based on where I had been and who I had been with—not on where and who I was with *now*.

I couldn't see the truth. I felt like there was no evidence of Ethan's love—and if I was even more honest, of God's. I didn't have a tight grasp of a love rooted in presence. I only knew the suffering that came from absence.

It's here, in this void, that we begin to form stories of who we are *in* the world and *to* the world. These stories shape how we see ourselves and how we perceive others to be.

Our stories wrap themselves around our hearts like a plant's roots in a pot, impossible to disentangle from until we choose to. Until then, we don't quite realize how suffocated we'd been, how imprisoned by our history.

In *The Myth of Normal: Trauma, Illness, and Healing in a Toxic Culture*, author Gabor Maté writes, "The world we believe in becomes the world we live in." He later goes on to say, "Our beliefs are not only self-fulfilling; they are world-building."[1]

What kind of world have you built for yourself? What kind of evidence have you been collecting?

I had created a world in which I could not trust those who said they loved me. I constantly needed affirmation to prove that it was so. I wanted to see it to believe it. But in order to move out of insecurity I had to believe I was secure. I had to be willing to take a leap of faith into the unknown. After all, "faith is the substance of things hoped for, the evidence of things not seen" (Heb 11:1 NKJV).

Could I learn to take my husband at his word?

More importantly, could I take God at his?

In the Bible, the Hebrew word *nes* is often translated as "banner," along with "ensign" and "standard." The banners described in the Bible were not what you probably envision when you hear the word. They weren't made of felt or fabric but were often figures or emblems made of wood or metal. They had to weather both travel and battle, and it was necessary that they were seen by all.

We see these words—*ensign, standard, banner,* as well as *signal*—used interchangeably throughout the Bible and historically, in mostly military contexts. Often banners were used as a rallying point for the armies they belonged to. They were a place to gather around or go out from. They often provided confidence and assurance to move into the unknown.

They were a silent promise to those who observed them.

Just as flags, jerseys, and uniforms do today, banners

signified several things for the people who carried them, including the following:

- Protection
- Authority
- Direction
- Reputation

Our stories, like banners, are more than just decorative. They point to what we've come to believe:

- Who protects us? Who represents us?
- Who stands behind us? What kind of power do we possess?
- Where are we headed?
- Do we live our lives from a place of wounding or healing?

Our stories can become templates we use time and time again to navigate new situations. They often guide us in processing conflicts, making decisions for future hopes and dreams, and connecting with others.

The stories we tell ourselves aren't so much what happened to us, but how we made sense of it—they're the conclusions that we came to as a result of our experience.

Here are a few that might sound familiar:

- Waiting is a waste of a time. No one will come.
- Because bad things happen to me, I must be a bad person.

- In the midst of the good, the other shoe is always bound to drop.
- To keep a relationship, I have to be perfect.
- I am easy to leave; I'm not wanted.
- No one cares for me, sees me, or really knows me.
- I can't ask for help because nobody will help me.
- I can't go easy on myself, or everything will fall apart.

These are just a few of the creeds that we might fall prey to when the banner of rejection casts its shadow upon our lives. Eventually, they aren't just stories to us—they become our ideologies. In short, rejection serves as an inferior guide leading us away from a life of confidence and into one of despondency. We become like who we serve.

We might see rejection, and the fear of it, manifest in us through procrastination, perfectionism, or a lifestyle of retreat—always running from what could bring us joy. We may refuse to ask for help or have a never-ending need for control.

We may constantly seek approval from others, and when we don't receive it, we withdraw or lash out in anger. We might find ourselves unsure of where we stand after a conversation—playing back every word in our heads after the fact. Every bit of our response is a representation of an unmet need, a longing we have that has been corrupted by our desire to self-protect.

My husband and I watch the Ultimate Fighting Championship (UFC) together. It has become a fun Saturday evening rhythm, a time to hang out and relax. We like to eat chicken wings, jalapeño poppers, and other delicious snacks while watching the UFC fighters essentially pummel one another.

Does that not sound like me? Honestly, I'm as surprised as you are.

I think what I love most about it is that these fights require more than just strength, dexterity, and training. It's more than just physical; it's mental.

Each fighter trains for months to prepare for only one night and one fight that usually lasts about fifteen minutes— unless it's cut short by a perfectly placed punch, kick, or chokehold.

UFC fighters are trained in an assortment of mixed martial arts, using tactics from boxing, wrestling, Brazilian jiujitsu, and Muay Thai, just to name a few. Though wrestling may be the foundational beginning for UFC, boxing is a close second, as these fighters spend as much time as they can in the center of the ring circling around one another, willing the other to strike first.

With boxing, you have to keep your hands up and stay on your toes. Both allow you to defend yourself while looking for any opportunity you might have to strike the other. If not, you're hit. I've seen too many fighters go down because they were caught off guard.

Maintaining this hypervigilance is exhausting. Though fifteen minutes doesn't seem like a lot, it's fifteen minutes of a full-body beatdown. It requires all of your focus. In the first round, these athletes are in their prime—they're fresh. Usually, they're able to withstand the first few minutes, even jumping into the second round with a lot of fight left. But the endurance it takes to keep this up eventually subsides, and even the best of them slow and tire, finding themselves struggling. Eventually someone gets pinned down or knocked out. Or if both fighters last all three rounds, the victory goes to whoever made the most strikes with the most damage.

In other words, it's unlikely you'll win with nothing but defense.

Our work to protect ourselves is not sustainable.

Eventually, we'll be pinned—all areas of our life impacted by rejection, abandonment, and betrayal. We'll tire out.

We'll feel the ache in our bones at all we lost out on because we only knew how to defend ourselves and not live life fully alive. We are unable to carry ourselves to wholeness and healing in the fight against rejection.

When faced with rejection, our responses become the beliefs that define it.

These beliefs create an inner world in which they rule and reign.

It's tempting to despise them or want to silence them. Though we often cast them as villains, these beliefs were formed to advocate for us. They are simply signals conveying a message and a need, and an invitation to bring them under the reign of a different standard of living—not by rejection any longer, but by Christ's instead.

Richard Schwartz, therapist and creator of Internal Family Systems, describes these responses and beliefs as "parts."[2] Schwartz argues that these parts are simply protecting us, trying to keep us safe, constantly tending to the emotions we hold from the most painful memories. These parts are constantly talking to us and attempting to guide us in whatever direction they feel is best for us. They often have good intentions, but with awful results.

They reinforce narratives that hold us back from living fully. Though these parts have served a purpose in our survival, we don't have to let them lead any longer. With Christ, we don't have to be led by just a part of ourselves, but by the Spirit instead.

To get here, we need to start by identifying these parts—or thought patterns and behaviors.

Schwartz's Internal Family Systems encourages us to move through these six steps:

1. **FIND.** Where do you notice a part of you that feels loud, that wants attention? What is it that you believe the most strongly? Sit quietly and see what comes to the surface.
2. **FOCUS.** Turn your attention to the part of you that seems the loudest. Stay curious to it. What sensations, thoughts, and emotions seem related to it?
3. **FLESH OUT.** What does it look like? Describe it. When did it first become a part of you? Does it dredge up a specific memory from your past?
4. **FEEL TOWARD.** How do you feel toward it? Do you find yourself feeling impatient toward it or uncomfortable with it? If you feel open to this part of you, you can continue on. If not, perhaps you start again—this time narrowing in on that part of you that began to protest.

5. **BEFRIEND.** Show kindness, compassion, and curiosity toward this part of you. Validate it. Maybe it needs comfort and reassurance instead of condemnation. Continue to ask questions that might help you understand it.

6. **FEAR.** What does it want for you? What does it want you to know? What is it worried will happen if it stopped doing or believing what it thinks it needs to?

Of course, we do not have to do this alone. As we walk through this visual picture of our inner world, we are empowered to bring these parts to the Spirit. As Jesus reminds us, "The Advocate, the Holy Spirit, whom the Father will send in my name, will teach you all things and will remind you of everything I have said to you" (John 14:26). The Holy Spirit can assist you in investigating those parts of you that are still living in the past and in the pain of rejection.

I've become accustomed to the language that these voices and desires are all *liars*. Yet I've shifted some of my thinking about that. While I understand the intention behind labeling them as such, we do a major disservice to ourselves by distancing ourselves from them in this way. We can't deny the truth that we have had experiences that reinforce these beliefs. Yet we also know that they aren't true all the time. Since they have been true at least once, they're worth listening to, not to confirm them but to validate the longings that lie beneath them. These beliefs come out of a desire to advocate for us, albeit often by unhealthy means. We miss out when we demonize and silence these inner voices. We know that their origins are maladaptive. But do we know that every misguided adage is a cry to be cherished, loved, cared for, and valued?

We don't have to live by these beliefs, but we can certainly tend to their needs.

Yesterday, I found the first book I ever wrote. I made it out of thick construction paper, each page carefully illustrated with markers or crayons. On the cover, I glued a picture of myself. I was in second grade. I'm wearing a yellow shirt with the school's mascot—a koala—on it. Back then, my hair was long, stark white, and I had large bangs my mom used to cut by placing a bowl on top of my head. She'd trim around its edges and—voila! It was fashion.

As my only daughter danced around me while I read the book to her, my attention stayed on the memory of this little girl who was just trying to make her way in the world. I returned to the cover, gazing into my own eyes, realizing that all these beliefs I held were to protect her. I wanted to keep her safe. I wanted to tell her she was loved—just as she was. I wanted somehow to fix a banner of truth permanently over her heart, pointing her to a life lived without fear.

I realized in that moment that she did the best she could. Do you need to hear that? You did the best you could.

I took that photo and taped it to the back of my journal. I didn't want to forget her. Now that little girl who needed to be held is held most tangibly. I bring her to the Lord time and time again, reminding her that despite everything, we're not doing it alone. And all the beliefs that had long taken care of her, they can live at peace. Another has stepped in: Jesus. His protection is steady, faithful, and unconditional. I remind her of that, when it's needed. I point her to this truth.

We are safe.

If searching your inner world for these beliefs feels too difficult, it might help to think of a time when you felt the most rejected or abandoned. Do you have a photo that represents that time in your life?

When you look at this photo, what do you see?

What does this version of yourself need to tell you?

What is it that this version of you needs to be free?

Has this version of you been brought to Jesus?

~

We can easily feel our wounds. But we can struggle to feel God working in our lives.

In Exodus 17, we see the Israelites fight against the Amalekites, who are intimidating foes. Moses stands atop a hill overlooking this battle with the staff of God in his hands. He acts as a signal to his men and, centuries later, for us too. As he lifts his hands, the men prevail, but when he lowers them, the Amalekites begin to win. Moses begins to grow tired, so Aaron and Hur flank his sides, helping him hold up his arms until the battle is won.

In honor of God and this victory, Moses builds an altar and names it "The Lord is my banner." Though Moses had the help of Aaron and Hur, he recognized that it was the presence of God that led them to overcome. God brought them through. In fact, it was by Aaron and Hur that the

Lord worked. He gave Moses strength by sending others to stand by him.

We can do the same in our own lives. We can look across the battle-weary territory in our hearts and build an altar. God's presence can become our banner too.

He sustains us. He carries us through.

Like Moses, we might also admit and accept that, at times, we need someone to hold us when we grow tired, when the load becomes too much. We need people who can support us and share their strength with us. Sometimes we need someone who can carry our story and hold it close.

Who might be willing to help us? Who already has?

At times when I felt like I couldn't rely on others, I fought to cling to the few people I could. I had my husband. I had a therapist. I had just a few friends I could trust. They could hold my story and me unflinchingly—curse words and all. I knew that without fail, they would point me to truth and to Christ. In them, I saw the presence of God.

Some days I would stand in the kitchen with my husband drinking a cup of coffee, once again reexamining the stories that still hurt. With my therapist, I would ask the questions I was too afraid to say out loud and share the worst of the worst. As for my friends, they'd patiently listen to my insecurities. I found comfort in their company.

Each of these places was safe—a space where I could see and be seen.

Eventually, you begin to believe what the people around you have been telling you. Where you might see a problem to be solved, they see someone who can be loved just as they are.

It didn't hit me until after a rather intense therapy session when my counselor asked me, "Tabitha, I wonder if you have always felt on the sidelines. Have you always felt like you didn't belong? And on the other hand, can you think of any time when you felt like you did?"

For a minute, I sat there thinking through the last three decades. I had always, it seemed, had a sense of not fitting in—of being excluded.

However, we talked about how, in many cases, my experience of rejection didn't always fit someone's experience of me. There were times when I would feel left out by a friend, only to call to ask her about it and find out it wasn't what it seemed. There were times when I would think someone absolutely hated me, and then I would be invited out to coffee by them later that week. It was disorienting. I couldn't quite make sense of it. When I looked long enough, an abundance of evidence showed that despite what I felt, I had actually been welcome and accepted.

In other sessions, we had been working through the idea that there was a strong possibility that I was neurodivergent. All that means is that I can experience the world differently than others, possibly due to undiagnosed ADHD.

She said to me, "Tabitha, it could be highly likely that because of the way your brain functions, you may have seen the world through a lens that doesn't always match its reality."

You don't have to be neurodivergent to have written a story about your life in which you're always rejected, never included, or never thought of. In fact, at every moment, we're all forming stories about the people around us, the experiences we have had, and the way it makes us feel.

35

But are they true?

I leaned back in my chair and didn't say anything. I was speechless. I hadn't ever thought of that. I had created this world I had been living in. And now that I could see it more fully, I understood that I could rebuild it. I could reclaim it. I didn't have to live my life this way—with this perspective—any longer.

This is the hope of Christ in our lives. He opens our eyes so we can see. Christ helps us see the way we have lived and now can live—rehabilitated and rewritten.

Jesus sets his banner over us and calls us forth into life, prophetically fulfilling Isaiah 11:10, "In that day the Root of Jesse will stand as a banner for the peoples; the nations will rally to him, and his resting place will be glorious."

We don't have to live at war with ourselves. Jesus, Messiah—the Root of Jesse—offers us rest. He offers us a place of peace after we've been hurt and disappointed. We don't have to work so hard to be loved. We don't have to try so hard to belong.

Beloved is the banner under which we reside. Belonging is its gift to us.

The Lord ushers us into an abundant life where we have everything we could possibly need. Song of Solomon 2:4 says, "Let him lead me to the banquet hall, and let his banner over me be love." Jesus rewrites our stories, one of power and love, and not of fear (2 Tim. 1:7).

We can introduce to Christ each belief that we hold that hasn't yet met Christ's love. And each of these parts can be given a new name, a new song, and a declaration of triumph:

Instead of ashes, a garland.
Instead of rejected, beloved.
Instead of forsaken, *his*.
Instead of mourning, the oil of gladness.
Instead of a faint spirit, a mantle of praise.
Instead of abandoned, held and embraced.
We become pursued, seen, and wanted.

Under these banners and in this story, we move into a place of healing instead of hiding in the shadows and instead of running away. We move out of misery and into confidence. These banners lead us into taking steps toward embodying the life, death, and resurrection of Christ in our hearts and hands.

Christ raises the standard for how we are to live. He raises this banner over us. And under this banner, we are grounded; we get to live at peace with ourselves.

To whom do we belong? Christ.

Whose power and authority stands behind us? The Messiah's.

Who directs our lives toward goodness and wholeness? The Lord.

We may have been divorced from those we love, abandoned by our family or friends, betrayed by the systems that raised us, but "though my father and mother forsake me, the LORD will receive me" (Ps. 27:10).

Christ carries the weight of our burdens. He will either send others on his behalf to hold us up or do so himself.

One of the first memories I have is of my mom and biological dad having an argument in our kitchen. I stood separated from them behind a baby gate. I felt alone and scared. The anger that filled the room disquieted me. I didn't understand what was happening between them.

For years, I would think of this moment frequently—without Jesus.

Everything changed when I brought Jesus into this memory.

I imagined myself as that four-year-old, tiny hands clenching the gate, eyes peering over the top of it at my parents. I imagined the discomfort I felt, and the confusion too. As I was imagining this, I began to look for where Jesus might have been in that moment.

Instinctively, I knew where he was. He was with me.

Jesus was kneeling beside me, one arm thrown around my shoulders. He wasn't looking at them but at me, as if to say, "I'm holding you."

Sometimes we have to invite Jesus intentionally into the places that feel the most alone. That includes our memories. Every time that I have, it has been profoundly impactful. It might be that way for you too. If you would like to try it, let me show you how it works.

Find a spot in your home that's quiet and comfortable. Close your eyes and take a few deep breaths. Imagine a memory that represents the part of you that hasn't met Christ, hasn't been led by the Spirit to wholeness, hasn't been seen, hasn't been made to feel secure and safe, and hasn't been soothed. As you remember, I want you to take a moment to look around.

Where is Jesus?

Maybe you ask, with prayer, that Jesus would help you to see where he was all this time—in a person, an opportunity, or the hope you had that gave you strength to push through.

He will show you.

We can know with confidence that Christ, our banner, was there all along.

INHALE

Lord, open my eyes to see
Your goodness and your mercy

EXHALE

Are forever and endlessly
after and with me.

BASED ON PSALM 23:6

CHAPTER 3

LOYAL IN HIS LOVE

W here are you from?" they'd always seem to ask. I would stammer, "Oh, well. I guess there's nowhere I'd call home." Such were the conversations I'd have with each move to another state. For a kid, I moved quite frequently. Every three years or so, my mom would receive orders from the military to pack us up and head out. It was and will be one of the markers of my character, teaching me things I would not otherwise know of myself and the world: tenacity, resilience, and adaptability to name a few. All of these and so much more came from this transient lifestyle. But for a little girl who already felt unseen and like she had to fight to be loved, moving so often only magnified these insecurities. I wanted to fit in, and I wanted to make friends—but I wasn't very good at that. I always felt a little behind and clueless about who I was supposed to be to belong.

My mom was doing her best. After my biological dad

left, my mom built us a stable life, one that she could manage on her own, with insurance, a steady paycheck, and security. The military offered us that support, but they required a sacrifice in return. In our case, it resulted in a deployment to Turkey. But of the 125 people who lived on that base, there were only seven other women besides my mom. No children. So since there wasn't a place for me there, I would not be able to go. It would be a difficult year for both of us.

My grandmother gave me a place to stay, with acres of land to explore while my mom served our country. Still, I was angry. A heaping mess of anxiety, I spent a lot of time at the nurses' office taking breaks from the constant sadness I felt.

I didn't have anything to keep me company. Not even conviction.

Every Sunday, my grandma faithfully attended a small Lutheran church and would bring me. But at that time, even though I knew God and had seen who God was, I felt in my heart that God had left me too. I don't know that I really ever thought God was there to begin with.

The truth is, we sometimes can't help but shape our beliefs about God in view of the absence and actions of others. We catalog the hurt as evidence that no one, not even God, can be trusted. We wrestle with who he is in our lives and his goodness—not that we believe that he isn't good, but we wonder whether he is, or can be, for us. We can see all that he has done for others, but when we look at our own lives, we're unsure whether he really cares. All we see is emptiness.

Our proclivity can be to pay attention to certain things

and ignore others, which is commonly known as attentional bias. We often only acknowledge those things that confirm the stories we already believe. Like most of what we do, this tendency springs from our survival mentality. If we pay extra attention to the things that could hurt us, then we can protect ourselves. But attentional bias can also affect our memories. Because we are so focused on one thing, we miss other, possibly more significant, details. We collect evidence to support what we believe, even if it's untrue. In pain, we become fixated on what has hurt us, and anything like it becomes its accomplice. We group things together that sometimes shouldn't be connected, our brains taking whatever shortcuts they can to speed through navigating the world. Our brains are naturally lazy,[1] and it's up to us to make them do the work they would rather not do—they need us to take personal responsibility.

So we must ask ourselves, "What am I paying attention to? What evidence have I been collecting against God?"

It's easier to do this work when you're surrounded by community, when people can show up for you and restore your faith in humanity—and maybe even in God. I pray you have such a community.

Christ moves through the body of believers, and when they show up for each other, it makes a difference. And yet we can't be spared from the disappointment that comes from imperfect people. They don't always know what to say. They don't always know how to care for you. They'll make light of the dark that feels like it's swallowing you whole. We also cannot deny the overwhelming amount of cases of serious abuse that we've heard about over the last few years.

So some of us have extracted ourselves from our communities. We've stepped away—for space, for time, and to alleviate the pain we've felt. Some of us simply haven't felt safe.

Because I have been where you are, it would not be fair to assume you feel seen or known by the body of Christ in the form of a community. You may not. And yet God can still meet you.

Even here.

I don't know how many times I've heard others say that we can only find hope and healing in community. Often it's disguised as a well-intended directive to join a small group or to serve as a volunteer. Sometimes it's a little less explicit as we simply see the happiness of those around us who have someone in their lives looking out for them.

Undeniably, we thrive when we have others.

Yet I believe God can meet us when we're alone too—just us, on the closet floor, laid out with tears streaming down our cheeks. We can know God's love even without the love of others. It's not ideal, but it's possible.

The intimacy we cultivate with the Lord in these moments fortifies our faith. It becomes our shared history with God—and come to find out, this connection can't be stolen or taken from us. It becomes the basis in which we see everything.

Our origin story doesn't have to begin with us, but with the character of the one who created us. The genesis of who we are and get to be can rest in the pedigree of our Father in heaven.

When we are rejected by people, we can begin to believe we have also been rejected by God. We might not believe God is for us. Maybe, like an absent earthly father, God seems to be against us.

Sometimes when we haven't dealt with rejection or abandonment directly, we can't help but project it onto God. It relieves the tension we might feel subconsciously, but it puts a wedge between us and God. We might miss out on what God has for us because we don't see him distinctly. We compound our issues by setting God against us, though God is not.

When we can unquestionably believe in who he is, separate from our experiences with others, we can grow generously. More importantly, when we're able to rectify our distorted view of God, we will be able to extract ourselves from the mistaken beliefs that adversely impact our relationships with others.

On my trip to Texas for my grandma's ninetieth birthday, I had a day to stop in Houston with my aunt Margaret and uncle Scott before flying back home to Colorado. Aunt Margaret is an artist, so it was no surprise when she asked if I wanted to visit a few of the local gems in the Houston Museum District: the vast and beautiful Menil Collection and its counterpart, the Cy Twombly Gallery. But what stood out to me most on our trip were two chapels. We walked over to the University of St. Thomas to visit what must be the most artistic and modern chapel I have ever seen, the Chapel of St. Basil. It was a large cube constructed of white stucco, topped with a golden dome. The doorway sits within a vertical rip, as if the wall is being torn apart, just waiting to be zippered back up. There are no interior lights. The sun shines through the dome illuminating every corner of the sanctuary.

When we walked in, I was surprised at how simple it was on the inside. Pews lined the room, almost filling it, and a platform sat at the front with six large standing candles and one table. To the side, engraved into the stucco, were poignant moments from the death and resurrection of Jesus Christ: the Stations of the Cross. Etched in the white walls in bas-relief to stand out from across the room, the images were compelling. Usually, Stations of the Cross contain fourteen images, but in this chapel, there was a fifteenth: an image of the risen Lord.

The bas-relief called to me. Its intricacies told the truth of not only Christ's life, but mine. It revealed God in his glory. Everything else faded away.

Later, we walked to visit the Rothko Chapel. My aunt refused to tell me what it was or what to expect, as it was meant to be an experience. As we approached, I could tell it was very different from the first chapel: a plain, octagonal brick building. We wandered in, and it was clear we were supposed to be quiet. No conversations were allowed. The entryway had a variety of different spiritual texts and books lined up, sitting together. We walked into the large, eight-sided room and found a spot on one of the long brown benches placed all over the room. It was dim. I almost felt as if I was being deprived—of light, sound, and meaning. This space was empty of theological truth, of any indication of who or what was meant to be worshiped.

On each wall were permanent paintings by abstract artist Mark Rothko—fourteen *massive* canvases covering most of the walls. Each canvas was painted in what appeared to be a muted black. In this room, I felt cut off from the world. The point of this experience is to sit and gaze at this art in order to meet it—or to let it meet you. After a while, the light, my eyes, or perhaps my mind began to peel apart the monochromatic canvases to see what appeared to be different shades of black. In fact, I was certain I could see deep purple.

This was a chapel left open to interpretation—to the visitor and to the heart. Every visit perhaps results in a different story, a different revelation.

What a clear difference between this chapel and the first.

The canvases don't have a story to tell, except the one you are already telling yourself. It seemed to operate as one big human projector, its content determined by its viewer.

I imagine this is much like our experience with God. At times we can live within the second sanctuary—painting images of who and what we think God must be from our memories or from how we are feeling in the moment. We paint him into our stories in that way, in who we think he is and how we perceive him.

Even though we should value and honor those experiences, we also must remember that God is not like us. Nor is he like other people. He is like himself, and as the Stations of the Cross in the Chapel of St. Basil remind me, his story is unique. It stands alone.

This one unchangeable truth is comforting.

God moves beyond the scope of our understanding. We cannot put him in a box.

⌒

What would it look like to grasp the evidence of who God is? How might it ground us? How might it restore our vision? If you're like me, perhaps it's easy to forget to whom we belong. Or maybe you haven't given yourself room to wrestle with the characteristics of God, relishing them so that they might cement themselves in the cracks of your faith. Where do you still have questions? Where do you still struggle to believe? Take note of any skepticism that materializes in you as we turn our attention toward God's heart. Let yourself linger where you might doubt.

Though there are many qualities that describe the one who created us, here are a few with special relevance to the topic at hand:

GOD IS ALL-POWERFUL

Jesus looked at them and said, "With man this is impossible, but with God all things are possible." (Matt. 19:26)

No wound is too deep, no heart too dead, no relationship too soured for God to bring transformation. And though there are obstacles to overcome, hurt that separates us from the lives we want to live, God can't be stopped. Knowing

God's power breeds hope in us. It frees us from believing we must save ourselves.

GOD IS EVERYWHERE ALL AT ONCE

Where can I go from your Spirit? ·
    Where can I flee from your presence?
If I go up to the heavens, you are there;
    if I make my bed in the depths, you are there.
If I rise on the wings of the dawn,
    if I settle on the far side of the sea,
even there your hand will guide me,
    your right hand will hold me fast.
        (Ps. 139:7–10)

When we've been betrayed or ostracized, we can hide from people. We can feel unseen, both physically and in our hearts. But we can't hide from the Lord. God welcomes us as we are.

GOD IS ALL-KNOWING

You have searched me, LORD,
    and you know me.
You know when I sit and when I rise;
    you perceive my thoughts from afar.
You discern my going out and my lying down;
    you are familiar with all my ways. (Ps. 139:1–3)

Every detail of every injustice, of every suffering, is in God's hands. God knows how we were wronged and how things didn't work out. God knows the desires of our hearts and every tear that's fallen. God's all-knowing nature isn't devoid of care. It's foundational to God's care for us. God holds every moment that's been broken and doesn't forget but instead redeems them.

GOD IS SOVEREIGN

Whatever the LORD pleases, he does,
in heaven and on earth,
in the seas and all deeps. (Ps. 135:6 ESV)

God reigns in our lives as Yahweh. We cannot escape from God's love or plans for us. Where we see limitations, God is boundless. Anything that must happen according to God, will. No plans devised by others or our enemy can thwart what God wishes to occur.

GOD IS RIGHTEOUS

The LORD is righteous in all his ways
and kind in all his works. (Ps. 145:17 ESV)

God operates in our lives with honor. God always does the right thing, with perfect timing and execution. God's righteousness is holiness in action. God upholds a moral standard, applying it to every moment, every circumstance. But because of Christ, we also get to live out righteousness. We no longer must strive or prove ourselves because Christ stands in our stead.

GOD IS JUST

He is the Rock, his works are perfect,
  and all his ways are just.
A faithful God who does no wrong,
  upright and just is he. (Deut. 32:4)

Do not take revenge, my dear friends, but leave room for God's wrath, for it is written: "It is mine to avenge; I will repay," says the Lord. (Rom. 12:19)

God will set everything right again. When we have been wronged, we desire justice. We want to see the people who have hurt us be held accountable, apologize, and admit their wrongdoing. Often we want this in the most public way; we want to be vindicated. God wants this for us too. And we can rest assured that this justice comes for all of us.

We could sit for weeks in each of these qualities, unraveling them and only barely understanding them. But that is the point. God's character is expansive. Have we taken the time to know it? Where it feels too difficult to understand, we're given the grace to grapple with God. We can ask God for revelation. And then still we may cry out, "I do believe;

help me overcome my unbelief!" (Mark 9:24). We may pray that God would stretch the limits of our knowledge and imagination. God's gift to us is this: the relief in knowing that God is not us.[2]

To behold God as set apart changes everything. A. W. Tozer writes,

> To admit that there is One who lies beyond us, who exists outside of all our categories, who will not be dismissed with a name, who will not appear before the bar of our reason, nor submit to our curious inquiries: this requires a great deal of humility, more than most of us possess, so we save face by thinking God down to our level, or at least down to where we can manage Him.[3]

I've learned that part of beholding God is being able to sit in mystery. I simply can't wrap my rational mind around God being in every place all at once. But I know God is with me, my husband, and my children. And still, simultaneously working in the lives of my neighbors, my enemies, and the strangers who sit in the car next to mine. I don't have to understand it to believe it.

There is comfort in control. After all, we say that knowledge is power. But when we suspend our need for comfort, we might step into the truth of who God really is by letting him be bigger than we could ever envision.

God is not an island in this world, but a world all God's own—a kingdom that stood down to bring us right-side up, to help us steady our hearts and find our way.

In Acts 17:24–25, we see this come to life: "The God

who made the world and everything in it is the Lord of heaven and earth and does not live in temples built by human hands. And he is not served by human hands, as if he needed anything. Rather, he himself gives everyone life and breath and everything else."

Who are we to play judge and jury? Why do we put God on trial for the failings that belong to others? How can we prosecute the one who in all perfection made us and the world?

I think of God's response to Job in the midst of his suffering:

> Where were you when I laid the earth's foundation?
>   Tell me, if you understand.
> Who marked off its dimensions? Surely you know!
>   Who stretched a measuring line across it?
>   (Job 38:4–5)

Or, in Isaiah, this admonishment:

> Who has measured the waters in the hollow of
>   his hand,
>   or with the breadth of his hand marked off the
>   heavens?
> Who has held the dust of the earth in a basket,
>   or weighed the mountains on the scales
>   and the hills in a balance? (Isa. 40:12)

Knowing the immensity of God puts rejection into perspective. God's authority puts rejection it in its proper place: beneath him. Though it may not calm the sting of the wounds that others have inflicted, when we put God at the helm, we can trust that these wounds will heal.

When we know who God is, we're guided not by the minor view we have of each other, but by the broad view we have of God.

When I was visiting my grandmother for her birthday, I decided to go for a run down the stretch of highway that sat at the entrance of her home and around a dirt road guarded by a herd of cows. As I ran, I noticed the wildflowers blooming, swaying in the wind and basking in the sun on the side of the road and in the ditches. Indian paintbrush and bluebonnets sprang from the ground wherever I looked. I could not escape them.

It struck me that this was confirmation of a God who was who he said he was. These wildflowers were more than just petals and leaves; they were a declaration of who I am and who all those who have been rejected are to him. Wildflowers plant and bloom without the help of anyone. They're tended to by creation, with a helping hand from the Lord. At times they are unseen and taken advantage of. But God sees them all. The way God tends to the wildflowers echoed all the traits I'd come to meditate on.

God is not us. But God is for us.

The wildflowers brought to mind more of who God was, just as important as the ones above:

GOD IS MERCIFUL

The LORD, the LORD God, merciful and gracious, long-suffering, and abounding in goodness and truth, keeping mercy for thousands, forgiving iniquity and transgression and sin. (Ex. 34:6–7 NKJV)

God won't leave us alone or abandoned. Though God could crush us, God chooses to preserve us. God gives to us abundantly, though there is nothing we could give in return.

HE IS FAITHFUL

If we are unfaithful,
> he remains faithful,
> for he cannot deny who he is.
> (2 Tim. 2:13 NLT)

When we are at our worst, God remains at his best. Our attitudes and actions cannot sway God from the conviction that we are God's, always and forever.

HE IS LOVE

And so we know and rely on the love God has for us. God is love. Whoever lives in love lives in God, and God in them. (1 John 4:16)

His love is what ties it all together. Love is what moves God, and God's presence into our lives—in the form of Jesus, then the Spirit. It is God's love that fuels the patience, kindness, and gentleness God has for us.

We can rest assured that God's faithfulness can't and won't be swayed by others' faithlessness. God's promises don't cease because other people broke theirs.

What God desires to give us is not contingent on what we have to give. And God's love won't change because we've done wrong.

God is not the people who have hurt you.

From Texas to Colorado, the wildflowers followed me. That summer, I saw what I would unofficially call a superbloom. In the two decades I've lived here, I've never seen so many wildflowers. They saturated every field and ditch, a crowd of witnesses made of yellow and red and purple screaming at me to notice them as I drove by.

I was learning to see God in the wildflowers. God's presence beckoned to me. In the middle of a discouraging season, God was reminding me that I wasn't alone.

Our attentional bias can just as easily be swayed to look for more positive stimuli.

So I intentionally started to look for the wildflowers. I began to collect photos of them, pulling over on the side of the road during errands and taking my family to the mountains just so I could be surrounded by them. My kids knew I was looking for them, and they began to look for them too, snagging as many as they could in their little hands, rushing up to me to show me their latest find.

I would bring them home and press them in between

the pages of my books, collecting each petal as if they were an epistle written from God to me. Each wildflower was a sermon declaring God as constant, and fulfilling every need I had in a period of unending loneliness.

If I could find evidence of lack, I was certain I could do the same for abundance—for the goodness of God, for his presence, and for the truth that God *really* was looking out for me.

Therapist Deb Dana coined a term that captures the essence of this concept, calling these moments "glimmers."[4] Glimmers are small moments of joy. They are points of reference in our days where we've seen beauty and felt hope; when we are fully engaged in what's right in front of us. Glimmers are when we feel calm and connected. Glimmers help regulate our emotional and physical states. They cue our bodies back to a place of safety, of refuge. They help us to reconnect. To God, even. To see God in the ebbs and flows of our life.

English poet Elizabeth Barrett Browning once penned,

> Earth's crammed with heaven,
> And every common bush afire with God,
> But only he who sees takes off his shoes;
> The rest sit round and pluck blackberries.[5]

Every wildflower is a declaration. Each one an invitation to reunite with God.

Every glimmer makes it clear that God is chasing after me. God is chasing after you too—not only through these pockets of beauty we find in the most abandoned of places, or in the laughter of our kids, or in that first sip of coffee in the early morning, but also in every shadow of our story.

Where? We just have to look.

I borrowed the format of Psalm 136 and saw that I could find God's pursuit of me in this way—I read the psalm and then made it my own. I interjected my story into every line.

> The God who was with me when my own father left me,
>> For his loyal love endures forever.
> The God who embraced me when I was alone,
>> For his loyal love endures forever.
> The God who was steady when nothing else was,
>> For his loyal love endures forever.
> The God who empowered me to be unlike the
>> legacies left before me,
>> For his loyal love endures forever.
> The God who received our tears when we lost our
>> first child,
>> For his loyal love endures forever.
> The God who was our refuge when the church
>> couldn't be,
>> For his loyal love endures forever.
> The God who befriended me when I was friendless,
>> For his loyal love endures forever.
> The God who saw me and provided for me when no
>> one else did,
>> For his loyal love endures forever.

Could you do this? Could you let the Lord reclaim your story?

You might begin by drawing a blank timeline on a page. Let this reflect the entirety of your life so far up to this moment. Starting from the beginning, reflect on those events that impacted you the most—both the good and the bad. For each, mark your timeline with a vertical dash. Let the more painful moments be delineated by a mark that points down, and the more delightful moments by a mark that points up.

Once you're done, take some time to look for how the Lord showed up.

What did he do for you? How did he help you through?

Then take what's left and insert it into the stanzas of Psalm 136 and make it yours.

He had always been there. In every nook and every cranny.

I can't get past the idea that ultimately, everything in my life and in yours didn't work out the way we hoped for. We wrestle with how a good God could let bad things happen to good people.

For me, I've come to find that resolving the problem of pain isn't so much the answer I need.

Instead, I've learned that it isn't so much what happens to me but rather knowing that God is with me when it happens. And because of his loyal love, I'm confident I will make it through. His love is all we need when there is nothing else that we can do.

When I struggle with my circumstances, before I blame

God or tumble into dejection, I simply ask myself, "What do I know of God's nature?"

Psalm 136 intrinsically describes the Hebrew notion of the *hesed* of God. Over and over, we see it state that God's loyal love will endure forever. However, *hesed* is such a difficult idea to nail down with a single word, so different versions of the Bible translate it in a variety of ways: "loyal love," "loving-kindness," "faithfulness," "steadfastness," "mercy."

It's *hesed* that shows us how much God is for us and with us. It is, significantly, not only how we describe the Lord, but also how he describes himself (Ex. 34:6).

Hesed is a covenantal love. It's not given based on what we deserve or earn. It's always available. Unconditional. God is bound to this love because it is the essence of who God is. Since God cannot betray his character, *hesed* isn't merely something God does; it's who God is. It's not simply the way God feels but how God acts toward us.

As with the wildflowers—those glimmers of assurance—we can begin to see the goodness of God, his *hesed*, in our stories. His goodness and mercy, the psalmist says, are chasing after us (Psalm 23:6). When we find beauty and experience joy, we're witnessing God's hands in our lives. And this is where we anchor our faith: in his character. It's looking beyond the lurid details of our past or a particular wound to the cellular level of it all, knowing that even as you felt broken, God was mending you. Or that by the grace of God, you got through. It's seeing the miracle of a sunset and rejoicing in the one who painted it. It's breaking your body on the back of a mountain as you trudge up it, knowing God is bigger. It's standing on the golden, course sand of a beach, believing that the sum of every grain is still less than God. It's taking in the sight of every living being around you and knowing they were made in God's image, every strand of their hair counted and every heartbeat accounted for.

"Taste and see that the LORD is good," the psalmist exclaims in Psalm 34:8. We're to look for *hesed*, to pry it from every detail of our lives and savor it. To stand in the presence of it and experience it. To relish in the glimmers of God's love.

If God sets a table before us, filled with delights of every kind, and asks us to sit down at it, what good does it do us to spurn it? What joy does it bring us only to watch as others eat?

David, the psalmist, challenges us not simply to take his word regarding God's goodness but to test it for ourselves. To dig in and fill our plates. God invites us to see him and to know him.

At first, we might only be able to taste a morsel of God's goodness. For all we know of him, we still see him dimly and in part. Each day is an opportunity to sample more of God. Every bite a hint at a more complete version of the lives we get to live, God's promises fulfilled.

When we take the time to become familiar with who God is, we see over and over again that God has never left and will never leave.

Priest Terrence Klein so aptly says, "The only one who can love all, without rejecting any, is God. That is what makes God, God."[6]

May we know the one who never forsakes us.

∽

As I am writing this book, the wildflowers I have clung to as signs of God's goodness are withering away. Dead stalks stand in their place, and they're being mowed down ruthlessly in the fields they have inhabited for months. Yet what I perceive as death is but an illusion.

Wildflowers are self-perpetuating. They will spread and reseed themselves freely. Life will spring forth time and time again.

In fact, Daniel Winkler, a USGS desert expert, is quoted in a *National Geographic* article as saying, "Even in the driest drought, deserts aren't wastelands, but a flower miracle waiting to happen. . . . The seeds that feed the blooms are always present in the soil by the billions, just waiting—sometimes for decades—for the right conditions."[7]

The seeds are always present, even when we can't see them.

Abundance is always there. It is always here—right under our feet.

Though I find myself rejoicing in who God is, I do still find myself stumbling, at times raising my fist at God in frustration when I'm disappointed by others—and even, it seems, by him. Maybe these times are less about proving that I know God fully and more about accepting that I don't.

God invites me to know more.

We can strengthen our hope on this: that the love of God

has seeded these lives of ours. Glimmers of God's goodness hide in plain sight. We just have to look for them. Even where we might feel the most parched, God will never fail to drench us with unceasing presence.

INHALE

Lord, you are my refuge and strength.

EXHALE

My ever-present help,
you are always with me.

BASED ON PSALM 46

CHAPTER 4

IN THE WILDERNESS

I'm sitting by a fire outside the cabin we've rented for the
weekend.

As a family, we make annual trips to the Rocky
Mountains as much as we can. We love Colorado. We love
that we can remove ourselves from the hustle and bustle of
life. It's here where we find rest and then leave restored.

While I take sips from my coffee, I examine the bare aspen
trees that surround me. Soon, they'll grow full of golden,
quaking leaves. But for now, their trunks and branches jut
into the skyline, marked by the insatiable cravings of the elk
and moose who rub them raw, and by the initials of hikers
in love. The aspens' bleached bark is covered in spots that
look just like eyes, peering out into the forest. Every ring
formed inside their trunk is a declaration of another year
and another tale to tell. And every tree is wired to the next,
everything intertwined, everything a part of the whole.

Dendrology, the scientific study of trees, tells us that trees are interconnected. They share water and nutrients through underground fungal networks. They even send messages via chemical, hormonal, and electrical signals to one another—about anything of distress.

Every tree is like us, our past and present and future forever joined together, chronicling, celebrating, and declaring what was and is and could be. Our past communicates with our present, alerting us to what might hurt us or reminding us of what already did.

In mass, trees can be unnerving. Encircled by them, we're not sure how to make our way through them. It's similar to how we might feel when we're pushed out, forsaken, and abandoned. We're left in the middle of nowhere. We're lost.

Like the aspen grove, we may struggle to separate ourselves from the things that have happened around us because of just how interconnected it all is.

Without realizing it, we can begin to embody our history. We live out our fears by means of a self-fulfilling prophecy. Our stories become more than just what happened to us; they become who we are. Our past doesn't just impact our present. It can, if we let it, determine our future too.

There are many ways to move forward into the future, but sometimes it's through the tangled web of limbs and boughs, where the path isn't so clear, that we must go. We must travel through the places that feel most forsaken to see that we are held. We must look at where we've been to determine where we'll go.

While we have named the pain, that isn't enough to heal

it. Yet it opens a way into the wilderness—or rather, a way through.

I've had to make a temporary home here in the wilderness. I have had to travel through every corner of my life worn thin by rejection, knowing that my past is ever-present, and knowing that making space for it will only empower me to align myself with a story told through the eyes of Christ and not my own. It's in the wilderness that we might lose ourselves, but where we also might discover restoration and renewal.

Long before it became a known epidemic, my husband and I found ourselves recovering from extensive emotional contusions made by a local church we'd given nearly a decade of our lives to. Our church had been our sanctuary and our refuge. It was our community.

Over the years, Ethan had worked many jobs for this church. At one time or another, he was the youth pastor, the college pastor, and the director of operations. We spent so much of our time and our lives in this building and with these people. We were enmeshed in it in every sense of the word. We dated, married, miscarried, and had two children while there. We were building our lives, our hopes and dreams, around this building.

Church didn't start to become a problem until the last three years or so. At first, we didn't mind throwing our whole selves into supporting the church. It felt commendable and holy. Ethan worked, and I volunteered and served wherever I could.

We saw our leaders as wise. In our eyes they could do wrong.

We looked up to them. We trusted them.

Then it all fell apart.

It wasn't just the seventy-hour workweeks or the constant phone calls from various people asking for assistance during our vacations and at all hours of the evening. It wasn't just that I had attended every Sunday service for the last few years alone because no one could relieve my husband of his responsibilities. It wasn't just the incessant pressure to make the church grow at the expense of the people who could only do so much. It wasn't just the way they asked for more but wouldn't provide the resources. It wasn't just the secrets we weren't supposed to know but did. All of it was awful.

Ultimately, the problem was that my husband was not valued. It seemed to me that he was just a cog in this faulty machine, replaceable and objectified.

Our leaders lived by the philosophy that diversity of thought was not tolerated—they valued not unity but uniformity. When staff members began to voice their frustrations, they were suppressed. They tried so diligently to make it work, until it all imploded.

My friend Jen bravely began the procession of resignation. She refused to tolerate the toxicity. She would not be abused by our church's broken system any longer. Then we watched as several of our friends and my husband's coworkers were picked off one by one, either by weariness or by sudden betrayal. We knew we had to get out.

In the meantime, I watched how our lives got smaller and smaller, as we were just trying to survive. My husband was drained, burnt out, and coping poorly with the burden of responsibility and expectations that were put on him. I didn't know how to help.

I had just delivered our daughter, Glory, into the world when we finally made the unwelcome decision to leave. But the pressure had already done a number on the both of us, and it was taking everything we had to keep our marriage functioning. We were barely holding our heads above water at a place that was supposed to offer refreshment and hope, not drown us in despair and exhaustion. We didn't have any support. We were left to fend for ourselves.

Ministry was killing us.

What do you do when what you thought was the safest place you had ever known turns its back on you, when home shuts its doors without a word, changes the locks, and pulls its welcome mat out from underneath your feet?

There's only one thing to do: You willingly make your way into uncharted territory. You invite the Spirit to become a map and compass. You let the Spirit direct you to the places you never thought you'd have to visit.

Ethan quit. It was time to leave.

On the very last Sunday we were there, I didn't know how to navigate the situation we had found ourselves in. The turmoil of the staff wasn't public. By all accounts, everything was fine. The turnover went unexplained. No one was talking about it. So we found ourselves having to pretend. I felt I had to lie about what was really taking place. It made me feel crazy, like I'd imagined it all.

After the service, a celebration was held for us and another couple who had been let go. There was cake, snacks, and drinks. It only made me feel all the more uncomfortable.

69

Our departures had been embellished with optimism, and the festivities organized under false pretense.

"We love them! But God has called them elsewhere."

Maybe that kind of worked for Ethan and me, but it didn't work for our friends.

It all just felt so heavy.

I didn't think hors d'oeuvres could ease our pain.

People drifted in and out of the room, saying their good-byes. Later, the head pastor and his wife came in to make the rounds. As they gathered everyone around them, they said a few seemingly hollow and forced words and then left. As the room cleared, it hit me that the last five years had been a complete fabrication. Most of these people had been strangers to me. I didn't think these relationships could last beyond this building. I wondered if everything I thought I knew hadn't been based in Christ, but in something else entirely.

We had given so much of ourselves to this church and, in return, my husband was given a half-hearted pat on the back and then sent on his way. It was as if we had never mattered—as if our only value was in how much we could give.

It all felt like a sham. And this ending was not at all what I expected.

What complicates this matter, for all who have walked this path, is that so many of the years we spent at our church weren't terrible. There were times when everyone seemed to operate in harmony and work well together. There were dinners and game nights and baby showers and weddings and an overwhelming sense of . . . family.

It's the memories that make it hurt all the more.

Those of us who left or were fired scattered throughout our city. For some time, we didn't connect or attempt to talk with one another. From our church, few reached out to us. We felt isolated and didn't know what to do or how to act. We had all these complicated emotions and unresolved issues and nowhere to put them. In fact, we didn't know we could talk about the things that had happened to us. No one had given us permission to.

In some ways, we were afraid to speak about it, even with each other. It felt confusing and strange to be so *against* what we had been so *for*. The church had made up such a significant part of our lives and even our identities.

Though we were the ones who left, I believed there wouldn't be a major interruption in our relationships. I was wrong. Despite the many relationships we had formed in that church, few remained. They dissipated alongside our membership. We were cast aside, used up and broken, weary and on the verge of collapse.

Instead, I believe we were ignored for the sake of loyalty.

Belonging seemed to be more about the building than the body. We were no longer a part. No longer cared for.

I often wondered if we had become pariahs who were avoided intentionally.

At a time when I needed the body of Christ most, I couldn't turn to them. They were the ones who had cast us aside.

For a long time after, Ethan and I wouldn't attend services on Sunday anywhere.

In practice, it is difficult to separate the body of Christ from the church building. When people who represented your faith reject you, it doesn't just knock you down. It can dismantle the whole system in which you had rooted your belief. But the Lord grants mercy. He gives grace for the length of time it might take to disentangle your faith from the people who encouraged it in you. Christ gives us permission to wander, to lament.

I don't think I could have said it then, but I can say it now: it wasn't until everything fell apart that I realized how much of my faith had been entrenched in a system and not in Christ.

I didn't realize how much of my belonging to the kingdom was reliant on the affirmation and validation of others.

I didn't realize that much of what I had learned about relationship and community had less to do with being beloved and more to do with working my way to love.

I didn't realize our church was building itself through the sacrifice of people's lives and not on the sacrifice of Jesus at the cross.

When I think about the wild, I think about what it looks like in the dark. I imagine the roaming animals, like Colorado mountain lions and black bears searching for food.

With every twig that snaps, uncertainty hovers around you. While in the wilderness, you can't help but be on high alert for all that might harm you.

For all the fear you might feel, it's in the wilderness where you can unmask. There's no time to pretend when you're trying to survive. When you're starving, you reach out to be fed. When you're thirsty, you're desperate for a drink. Nothing else but the true thing can satisfy.

You would eat your own arm to survive.

You would burn your own clothes to stay warm.

The wilderness takes away all pretense and all performance. It unravels all the things you believed had to be true. It brings into striking clarity what matters most.

Rejection brings us into the wilderness.

But it's here that you get a full scope of your needs. You have a chance to ask questions like: What needs were you trying to meet? How were you trying to meet them? How did this relationship or dream consume or confuse you?

Did you find that you put all your hope in them?

Have you confused your pastor for your God? Your small group for the Holy Spirit? That opportunity for your savior? Your friendship or job for your identity and sense of security?

In whom or what, exactly, did you find your refuge?

I grew up running through the aisles of sanctuaries. My mom served as a chaplain's assistant in the Air Force for most of my childhood, and together we spent a lot of time at church. I'd meet her in her office after school, and in the summer I'd often spend full days there. Sometimes I'd take over the conference room and my mom would bring in stacks of VHS tapes for me. I'd watch *McGee and Me!* and *Adventures in Odyssey.* Other times, I'd pretend I knew how to play the organ, slamming my fingers on keys that wouldn't play, or I'd stand at the pulpit to deliver a sermon. I took naps under office desks, did homework, and discovered how delicious a fried bologna sandwich could be thanks to one of my mom's kindest colleagues, Cliff.

I always felt welcome. I always felt safe. I was home.

Church was a refuge.

But somewhere along the line, I twisted what it meant to belong with being able to contribute something. I implicitly believed there was a checklist that had to be checked, requirements I didn't quite understand, a level of performance I was trying to achieve but couldn't quite grasp.

Often I found that I desired the love of people more than the love of God.

For most of my life, the church building had been a sanctuary. But then the people who represented that sanctuary and inhabited it hurt me.

The word *sanctuary* comes from the Latin *sanctuarium.* *Sanctus* means "sacred" and "holy." It's where the altar is placed, where people can honor God with their offerings. A sanctuary is *meant* to be a refuge, a place set apart.

In their own long wilderness, we read that the Israelites set out to build a sanctuary and an altar for themselves and for God—specifically, the tabernacle, what was designed to be the earthly dwelling place of Yahweh. They took great care to construct it just so. Made of acacia wood and overlaid with gold, this sanctuary was designed to be portable. It was a tent. It's entrance was enclosed with blue, purple, and scarlet linen. It was elaborate, and it was specific.

After it was built, the glory of God rested upon it, as demonstrated in the appearance of a cloud above it. As the Israelites traveled through the wilderness, the cloud became their compass, its rise and fall serving as a signal of whether the Israelites should travel further.

In many ways, we create our own sanctuaries to serve as guides. We construct them just so—with our expectations, agendas, and rules—in hopes that the glory of God will rest upon us.

At times, we construct our sanctuaries on the bodies of those who serve instead of on the body of Christ who died. We expect our salvation to come from and through the people of the church instead of the head of the church, Jesus Christ.

As Dietrich Bonhoeffer wrote in *The Cost of Discipleship*, "When Christ calls a man, he bids us come and die."[1] But this death is meant to be consecrated to the Lord, not to build a building with as many people as can be stuffed inside—for the sake of prosperity or perception. Death to self is in resistance to the pressure of the world, not in giving oneself up for it.

When we must leave a church community, or if we cannot stay, it can feel as if God too is leaving us. It can feel as though we offered our lives only to see them buried under the building, trodden over, kicked in the dust. What we thought was our refuge was only a mirage.

But we cannot forget 2 Corinthians 6:16, which says,

"For we are the temple of the living God. As God has said, 'I will live with them and walk among them, and I will be their God, and they will be my people.'" Then in verse 18 God reminds us, "I will be a Father to you, and you will be my sons and daughters, says the Lord Almighty."

Where the Israelites were commanded to build a temple, we're blessed to have become one.

Our refuge lies within. God is with us. And though we may have been left to wander the wilderness without a procession of people to accompany us, we can make an altar in the recesses of our hearts and know that God will still teach and guide us.

In whatever way we might find ourselves separated from either a church building or it's people, we can still retreat to the haven of God's mercy and presence without fear.

Even though my husband and I have resumed attending church services, I still feel as if I'm wandering through the doors of our current church as if it were a wilderness.

Sunday is still often one of the loneliest days of the week.

I'm greeted by those who know my name but don't know me. We're working on it. I've believed for so long that I'd be hurt again, that I've become hypervigilant. It's hard to let others in, so I unintentionally hold them at arm's length, preoccupied with avoiding anyone who could be a threat.

It's strange to feel the friendliness of others but not know their friendship.

When I enter our church's sanctuary, I sit in the usual spot, and the darkness of the room enshrouds me. The melody of the worship pastor's guitar urges me to stand, and as I sing, I finally feel connected. All of our voices raise in tandem, belting the lyrics of familiar, intimate songs, weaving us together in ways that are hard to understand. Worship is the throne room where the King of Heaven sits, and we're all together meeting him there despite our differences.

The wilderness still runs straight through me, but I'm assured that I'm still one with the body of Christ and his church. Nothing can separate me from them, even my own misgivings.

There's grace for the time it might take to *feel* like you belong.

In this time, loneliness might set in. But I can assure you, you are *not* alone. If Sunday feels like a masquerade, and you're the only one unmasked, I know that feeling all too well. You might feel different, exposed even. You've come to terms with the idea that you might not meet the expectations of others. As they can't and won't meet yours. You know they won't always pursue you. You know they won't always check in on you. So how do you keep on?

What are your options in the wilderness? How do you press into the body of Christ when the people who form it feel so far away and challenging to connect with?

We learn to lean on the presence of Christ.

I wish I could give you some sort of practical guide to survive the scorched terrain in the wilderness, but there is none but dependence.

In Deuteronomy 1:31, we're reminded of how the Israelites moved through their own desert: "In the wilderness. There you saw how the LORD your God carried you, as a father carries his son, all the way you went until you reached this place."

When Ethan and I had our first child, Nash, we were nervous about leaving the hospital. When they told us it was time to go, I laughed and nervously asked them, "Are you sure we can take him home?" And then I panicked: "What will we do without you?" We lived only ten minutes from the hospital, but Ethan drove five miles an hour down the road. He braked as gently as he could, turning corners with care, unwilling to rock Nash so much as an inch. At every light, he slowed in anticipation of it turning red. Finally, he pulled into the driveway with a sigh of relief that reverberated down his whole body. I swear, beads of sweat pooled at the corners of his forehead, such was the concentration and attention it took for him to bring us there.

This, I am certain, is God the Father, a parent so careful with his children when they're weak and vulnerable, so aware of their helpless state and how completely dependent they are on him. He carries them like Ethan drove us home, focused on the destination but gentle in the journey.

I sat in the back of our car with Nash, my body pressing into the side of his car seat. I was prepared at a moment's notice to care and comfort him if he felt discomforted by the drive.

As with any small child, there's no expectation for us, no task we must accomplish, no deed that's required. We're buckled safely in God's grace and cradled in the hands of

God's mercy. Those on the outside may judge and criticize, especially if they've been through it themselves. They may honk in exasperation, calling to us to get a move on, to hurry, to get over the pain and the suffering. But the timing is not up to them to decide; it is between God and us. We know that God will keep driving us home, tenderly keeping his gaze on us, mothering us in the back seat. God's hands cradling us though we're buckled tightly to our seats.

With God there's always time to take it slow.

The church we used to attend is quite large. Through the wonders of social media, we can see in our periphery what the church is doing around and in our city. When I stumble upon a post that shares an event or story about them, it stirs up emotions within me. Sometimes I feel a sense of guilt that I've done something wrong by leaving them. It plants a seed of doubt that I'm less than because I don't demonstrate my faith the way they expect.

Am I less holy or less righteous?

One week, both Ethan and I were having a bad day, so in response, my husband texted a friend for prayer. In turn, the friend recommended that he should join an event our old church was hosting: "You'll find Jesus there," He said. His friend didn't mean any harm, but the comment stung and caused us both to swirl in doubt.

Was Jesus not *here*? Had he left us when we left the church?

Where is Jesus anyway? Is he at a big tent revival? Is he

in the largest church? Does he only work alongside the best-known pastor? Is he only with us on Sunday mornings or Wednesday evenings?

I don't know where you're at as you read this book, but would you try this with me?

Close your eyes.

Allow yourself to notice your senses.

What do you smell?

What do you feel?

What do you hear?

What are you touching?

Inhale and exhale, feeling the life being generated in you from your lungs breathing and from your heart beating, circulating blood throughout your body. Anchor your feet into the floor and your back against your chair.

Place your hand on your heart. Feel the weight of it sink into your chest.

And then as you breathe deeply, say to yourself, "Christ is with me. Christ is in me."

Jesus is here. He dwells within you.

Jesus is here. In your kitchen. At your desk. In the middle of your morning commute. In the confines of your hospital room.

On Sundays, even if you happen to be at home that day. You carry him with you.

You have become his dwelling place. Your life—every nook and cranny of it—is a holding place for his immense love and grace and mercy and compassion.

In the wilderness, you could be as close to home as a turn of the corner, but you wouldn't know it because you can't see. I don't know when the wilderness might end for you. So rather than tell you how to come out of it, I can point you to the thing that will sustain you: Christ's presence.

In the wilderness, we can hear the voice of God speak to us, beckoning us closer to the promised land.

And he does speak tenderly to you. God doesn't chastise or condemn you. He comforts you.

In the wilderness, all of what you hold dear is clarified for you continuously. You cross over from the place where you felt lost and dead to the promised land—rather, to the promised *one*. You are stripped of presumption and pride and bitterness and resentment and self-pity and anger, and you get to embrace acceptance.

We want to plow the desert and find fruit. But that's not our job. Let God do this work. Because unlike us, he is able to see good in fallow land. He sees good in our forsaken and betrayed hearts. Where we want to burn the land, he's ready to till it.

Our hearts are uncharted terrain. Only God knows their beginning and ending. He's intimate with the in-between. It doesn't scare him.

In the meantime, the wilderness dismantles any expectations you'll find salvation in other people. People are likely to disappoint, to change, to misinterpret, to misunderstand. In the wilderness, we learn that God is steady. God isn't always loud, but God is always there.

Might it be helpful to move from constantly needing to hold on to God to instead realizing you are held by him? You don't have to know where you are going. You don't have to categorize what God is doing. You don't have to perform here. You can show up as you are, as your heart is: desolate, weary, and afraid. You can be comforted by the simple truth that it was never your ties in this world that secured you; it was God.

Though we don't know what's on the other side of this emptiness, we can be certain of this: the wilderness isn't the end; it's a bridge.

The wilderness is a bridge we walk over, from sorrow to promise. From exile to belonging. From the margins to the center of God's heart.

We don't walk it alone, and we don't have to walk it without hope.

Where no one sees us, Christ holds us.

The wilderness sits at the seat of his love.

Pastor and evangelist F. B. Meyer once wrote, "It is necessary that God should have room in which to work: emptiness to receive him; weakness to be empowered by him."[2]

Our emptiness and weakness aren't deficits. They are gifts.

Though the wilderness can be unsettling, it is a place set apart for us to find refuge. It's where our hearts are refreshed. It's where our paths are reset. It's where we are primed to be filled with God's presence.

It's where our devotion is set on Jesus, and only Jesus, once more.

We're able to set down all of what we were never meant

to carry. We're stripped of what wasn't holy or righteous. He prepares in us ample room to receive him fully.

Christ won't let us stay wandering. He's making a way for our flourishing.

INHALE

Peace; Christ leaves with me.

EXHALE

Peace; Christ gives to me.

INHALE

Peace; Christ sustains me.

EXHALE

Peace; Christ makes me whole.

BASED ON JOHN 14:27

CHAPTER 5

GRAVEN IMAGES

I sat down at a round table in a darkened gymnasium, surrounded by women I didn't know. We had been hopping
from church to church for the last two years, eager to find
a new community while still tending to our wounds. On a
whim, I decided to sign up for a Women's Night at a church
we'd been trying for some time.

The activities of that night rushed around me while I sat
frozen. I felt apprehensive as I bristled at certain phrases the
speakers would say. But then the speaker panel grabbed my
full attention.

I honestly can't remember the question that was asked
or who exactly answered. I do remember that a woman
answered. Earlier, she had shared her story and testimony.
She talked about getting hurt—by whom or what, I don't
know. But something she said changed me profoundly.

She talked about how we often misplace our expectations

when we consider where our healing comes from. We spend too much time looking for something to happen between "us and them" rather than looking for something to happen between "us and God." As we heal, we need to move vertically, not horizontally.

I was stunned. I realized that I had been putting my faith in the wrong place, and my heart in the wrong hands. It hit me. This is what had caused so many of my problems to begin with.

In hindsight, I can see clearly how we tried so many ways to heal from our last church. We attended a house church, a small and untraditional church that met in a school, and a church that felt almost the same as the one we left, but much younger and hipper. I somehow expected to fit back in. I thought maybe being with other people would soothe my soul.

Instead, my body felt constantly activated—triggered—by the system that had hurt us. I wanted to fight. So I acted critical and cynical. At times, I felt apathetic and just didn't want to commit—to Sundays or any other kind of event. It was hard to show up consistently, or sometimes even at all.

Once, after dropping our kids off in a children's ministry at a church we had visited, we stood outside arguing over whether we should have come in the first place. Long after the service had started, we turned back, grabbed our kids, and headed home. We were angry and disappointed, fighting each other instead of focusing on the true mess: our hearts.

I realized that attending a different church wasn't the solution. Changing our setting was meaningless if we didn't take the time to mend what was on the inside too.

God was busy trying to bring our attention back to him, but we were so focused on changing what was around us. Sometimes, before we can be restored to others and see our relationships repaired, we must first reconnect with and be reconciled to God.

Let me be clear: our process doesn't have to be yours.

We needed to take time away, but you may not need to. Some people can remain where they are and simultaneously do the work on the inside. We're all different.

But I think many of us need permission to say, "It's okay to step away for a minute."

For me, I had to leave the church building in order to return to it.

Because we know God's character, we know there is room for us to breathe. There's no need to defend God or the misguided people who love him. We don't have to perform.

During our self-imposed break, I realized I had spent more time idolizing the nature of all my other relationships than focusing on the one relationship that never changes.

We could have gritted our teeth and tried to stay. We could have forced ourselves to attend. We could have completely stepped back into our old roles and same rhythms. But we didn't want to repeat what we had walked away from. More than grit, we needed the tender care of a God who saw us through Christ and not self-righteousness. We didn't have to pretend with him.

Before we could see our lives move forward, we would

have to tear down those things that stood in opposition to God: the idols that served as obstacles. And before we could move into wholeness, into healing, we had to dismantle the gods we had made of the people in our lives.

I want to be as gentle with you as I had to be with myself. I want to make it clear that when we are rejected, betrayed, and abandoned, it is not an issue of *fault*. I am not blaming you or me for the pain we've experienced. However, I believe some of this pain, if not all, is bolstered by our proclivity to place our hearts solely in fickle human hands.

I certainly wasn't to blame for my father leaving, but I made his absence more important than the presence of God. I swirled in doubt over who I was because of who my biological father couldn't be.

What we might call idols are just people and places and dreams that become more than what they actually are. They become spiritual forces, massive in our lives and the means by which we look for blessing, help, hope, or guidance. They become what we treasure, what we hold close, and what influences us to act. They become what we serve. Idols are dangerous because we attach our confidence, loyalty, and devotion to them. We become deceived by them, and we try to use them to fulfill our needs and desires.

This is where, in many ways, we are complicit in our own recurring pain.

Complicit may feel like a strong word, but when you look at its origin in Latin, it softens it's impact. Complicity means "to be folded together," to become so close to something or someone that we lose sight of where we begin and they end—or where Christ belongs in it all. Things blur together, and they become hard to separate from one another.

I couldn't separate Christ's love for me from the work my husband and I did for the church. In my failed friendships, I couldn't separate my belovedness from my belonging. For years, with my dad, I couldn't separate who he wasn't from who I was allowed to be. And in all things, I felt like the harder I worked, the better everything would be. I relied on me.

I wanted the church, my friends, and even my brokenness to save me. I tried to save me.

We're complicit because instead of serving God, we serve buildings or relationships or ideas. We carve our image—our identities—from these instead of leaving them at the cross. They take up space in our lives and in our hearts. And depending on the relationship, we can look to be either affirmed by them or validated by them.

But we serve a jealous God. And he commands us in Exodus 20:3–5, "You shall have no other gods before me. You shall not make for yourself an image in the form of anything in heaven above or on the earth beneath or in the waters below. You shall not bow down to them or worship them."

God knows that idols take us away from a wholehearted reliance upon him. Though we don't carve images into wood or metal and worship them quite like people did in ancient biblical times, we can easily point to many "gods" we are tempted to worship, ones we have built with our own hands.

Timothy Keller, in his book *Counterfeit Gods*, explains idols this way: "An idol is anything more important to you than God, anything that absorbs your heart and imagination more than God, and anything that you seek to give you what only God can give."[1]

That description is worth unpacking and examining. If we take a second to think through our actions and thoughts in relation to what's around us, we might discover small idols reflected in some of our most ordinary choices. It takes time to discern what we're living for, but it's worth a try.

Where do we hold back?

Where do we feel the least like ourselves? Or with whom?

To whom do we always say yes, even if we disagree?

Sometimes the answer lives within our worst fears. So we might ask:

Can I go without _____ today and not dwell on _____'s absence?

Would _____'s absence make me feel hopeless or even angry?

Can I lay _____ down without feeling the impact of it?

Does _____ have a major influence on the way I feel and think about myself?

Perhaps, like me, you must revisit these questions. We can easily reset and put God first.

It's not impossible to move away from our idols.

Our lives don't have to be shaped by these graven images.

⌒

In the Bible, Gideon is known for a variety of accomplishments. He was a military leader, a judge, and a prophet. While his story sadly ends in hypocrisy, it begins with faithfulness. In Judges 6:25–28, the Lord asks Gideon to pull down an altar of Baal, cut down the Asherah pole beside it, and build an altar to the Lord on top of the stronghold. Problem was, these were the altars that his father built.

Baal and Asherah were pagan gods that people often worshiped concurrently with Yahweh. Yes, we tend to marry our idols to God. They can be so folded together that we don't really know one from the other. We can't see that we are justifying the idol because we still worship God in its midst.

The graven images we worship these days are less tangible than the ones back in Gideon's day. Graven images are simply objects carved from wood or stone, erected plainly for all to see.

Yet the altars in our hearts are often obscured by good intentions. According to Diane Langberg in *Redeeming Power*, "As God's people, we are susceptible to being deceived by what we see, what we long for, and what we name good."[2]

Money, for example, provides—so we work for it. But it can often become more than just a means to an end; it can become our whole purpose. We hoard it. We abuse it. We don't know how to live life without copious amounts of it. When we don't have it, we panic.

Gideon is directed to tear down the idols and set up

an altar to God at the stronghold. Strongholds are places of defense and protection. So it makes you wonder: How often do we use our idols to safeguard us? After all, we typically don't erect idols out of malice or ill intent, but with an intense desire to fill our unmet needs.

So in fear and under the cover of night, Gideon and his men did as God instructed. They cut down the wooden pole of Asherah, fed it to the fire, and broke down the altar of Baal.

It was swift, drastic, and misunderstood. Yet it preceded everything else Gideon would do. After Gideon's obedience, the Lord clothed him with the Spirit and eventually led him to victory. The idols stood in the way of Gideon accomplishing what God had set him out to do, of both his potential and purpose.

When we set idols in our life that take the place of the Lord we may miss out on what the Lord has for our us. We must dismantle the misplaced power idols hold over our hearts.

Gideon gives a glimpse of what we must do. We must lay down those things we have put above and before the Lord and offer them up on an altar of our own. We might have to tear down

> our proclivity to please others,
> our fear of what others might think of us,
> our need for validation,
> our desire to belong more than to do what is right,
> our certainty that saving comes through service, or
> an identity that is anchored in friendships, parenting, marriage, or work.

We have to burn the reeds of performance and our desire for approval and break apart the expectations that hang heavy in the air over us. We protest and resist anything that is less than Jesus. Though it's uncomfortable, inconvenient, and even combative, it helps us reclaim our portion. We're able to embody Psalm 16:5, which reads, "Lord, you alone are my portion and my cup; you make my lot secure."

We give away what we want to keep because it makes room for the certainty of God.

Often idols can be our misplaced emphasis on things that are, by themselves, good. For me, it was, for a time, the church as an institution, religion, and its complicated idea of ministry. It was also sometimes the friendships that held me afloat for years. I did not have a healthy relationship with either, so I had to reorder my priorities so that I could come back to Christ.

St. Augustine, an early Christian theologian, described mixed-up priorities as "disordered love."

We desire good things, so we spend our lives chasing after them and being formed by them. Still, we're left empty and disappointed. On Augustine's concept, Timothy Keller captures it well when he says, "Disordered love leads always to misery and breakdown. The only way to 'reorder' our loves is to love God supremely."[3]

Idols are obstacles. They're barriers that prevent us from seeing God, from seeing how he wants to work in our lives. But because they often give us what we want, we become complacent—and complacency often leads us to complicity.

We may feel helpless or outright refuse to relinquish the false sense of security our idols have offered us for so long. The retribution might seem too catastrophic.

When we left our church, and after the anger subsided, it became clear that I had been shaped and formed not by the Lord but by an organization. I did everything I could to belong there. My relationship with Christ was based on my connection to this community—to the mission, to the sermons on Sunday, and to our success. I wasn't serving *God*. I was serving *them*. I wasn't forming myself to Christ; I was forming myself to what I was told was the best way to live and act and be.

No wonder I felt so empty when I sat in service on Sunday mornings. I was looking for validation and acceptance rather than freely worshiping. I had prioritized the one over the other.

A few years after we left our first church home, we settled into another. I was still healing and still doing the work of letting it all go. I was still not completely aware of where I expected others to provide, but where only God could.

I found myself getting offered leadership opportunities, which felt empowering. I couldn't believe that I was somewhere that really wanted to include me, even offering me a job and involving me in decision making.

I kept saying yes to those opportunities, not stopping to ask myself, *Why?* Under the guise of ministry, these all seemed like very good things. But I was more in love with being seen than I was with service. I cared more about what I could get than what I could freely give. I did what I thought I had to do to satisfy others' expectations of us.

I did what I thought was necessary to keep the peace and the status quo.

I could justify my actions as a means to an end: I was doing it all for God. It seemed to me that performance was the key to thriving at this church. If you didn't perform, then you were excluded.

When we eventually left, rumors abounded about us. Later, we were told that we should have communicated better—that even though we were struggling, it was on us to ask for help and support. To some extent, they're right. But we were unraveling, and we didn't need to be told to do more. Like everyone else, we were navigating through COVID and struggling with its impact on us as a family. Once again though, I felt as if I had been let down.

It was at this church that I had felt a flame of hope. I had made friends with a few women who were thoughtful, wise, and creative. And I was excited at the possibility of what these new friendships could become.

When we left, these friendships faded. They fizzled out without much fanfare.

To say the least, it hurt to go through this again. In hindsight, I'm grateful. It was at this point that I realized that something needed to change in *us*. Something was off, and we had to address it. I sensed it was time to confront our idols and muster the courage to say, "Enough."

Church culture had become the judge and jury of my identity. Its people got the final say.

I know this might sound irreverent. I don't mean it to be. I mean to point out that even good and decent things can overwhelmingly take the place of the Lord's authority in our life.

∽

The graven images—of security, power, influence, and loyalty—couldn't keep us safe. They are fallible, frail, prone to aberrate, and only eager to serve themselves, not others. I could give and give, and they would never be able to give back, nor hold me.

Psalm 115:4–8 says,

> But their idols are silver and gold,
>   made by human hands.
> They have mouths, but cannot speak,
>   eyes, but cannot see.
> They have ears, but cannot hear,
>   noses, but cannot smell.
> They have hands, but cannot feel,
>   feet, but cannot walk,
>   nor can they utter a sound with their throats.
> Those who make them will be like them,
>   and so will all who trust in them.

Habakkuk 2:18 asks us to consider, "Of what value is an idol carved by a craftsman? Or an image that teaches lies? For the one who makes it trusts in his own creation; he makes idols that cannot speak."

We know full well that people and the things they build disappoint. We cannot act surprised when the systems to which we entrust our lives break or when the people we believe are flawless can't live up to our expectations.

Idols can't shepherd us. Unlike Jesus, they won't leave the ninety-nine for the one.

These things we put our hope in will never give us what we need, though they will for a short time satisfy what we desire. They'll always leave us wanting for more. Usually, they will require that we leave our bloodied bodies in their calloused hands. In Charles Spurgeon's *Morning and Evening* daily devotional, he writes, "Nothing teaches us about the preciousness of the Creator as much as when we learn the emptiness of everything else."[4]

When we put our life in Christ's hands we become fully alive. We become full. Whole. Complete. Death means something to Jesus.

So it is at this altar that we meet him.

Recently, I finished reading the novel *Hinds' Feet on High Places* by Hannah Hurnard. My friend K.J. gave me an illustrated version to accompany me through what has been a bleak and demanding season. Hurnard tells the story of Much Afraid, a woman who so desperately wants to move from the Valley of Humiliation to the High Places where the chief Shepherd and King lives. It's a story that vividly captures the life and the imagination of a Christ follower.

Much Afraid's journey isn't easy. It's rife with visits from her nemesis and betrothed, Craven Fear, and her cousins: Pride, Resentment, Bitterness, and Self-Pity. She travels through the desert, the shores of loneliness, and the forests of danger and tribulation with her companions, Suffering and Sorrow. At various points in the path, Much Afraid is encouraged by the Shepherd, who steadily compels her forward even when she wants nothing more than to turn back.

At end of almost every perilous moment or encounter with the Shepherd, Much Afraid creates an altar, represented by a stone and accompanied by a declaration. Each one is a promise to the Shepherd that she will yield her will and her way in order to encounter and obey his.

Altars are where things are slaughtered.

At the start of her journey, when she's unsure of where she's heading, Much Afraid must trust that the Shepherd's will for her is good. "There Much-Afraid built her first altar on the mountains, a little pile of broken rocks, and then, with the Shepherd standing close beside her, she laid down on the altar her trembling, rebelling will. A little spurt of flame came from somewhere, and in an instant nothing but a heap of ashes was laying on the altar."[5] She denies her desire to follow her fears, to trust in what she knows, and puts away her self-reliance and her independence. She commits herself only to him. She sees that she has not once been able to provide what she's needed, but with hope, she trusts that the Shepherd can.

What would it look like to lay down our idols—the people we fear, the systems that disappoint us, the relationships that are faulty—at an altar like this?

We worry what might come to pass if we put our whole trust in the Lord, in the Shepherd. But we can follow him confidently because he does not lead us where he cannot go or safeguard us. Even when it seems to contradict his promise. Even when we feel as though we move forward empty-handed, and without a plan. We don't know what is around the bend. We can't know how others will respond to us. But the Lord gives us all that we need to endure.

The graven images we've constructed in our lives must be laid down. Daily, we must die to these. We must lay down our desire to save ourselves by our own means. We must bring to the altar other people's opinions, long-engrained beliefs of what keeps us safe, desperation to be understood and known, hope that we might be more than we are, and pride that we can take care of ourselves when others can't.

I must regularly remind myself that the world's view of me means nothing compared to the Lord's. Whatever the world has to offer me—comfort or control or influence—won't require less than myself. For these things, I will have to sacrifice my very personhood—who God made me to be, And none of that is worth a false sense of security.

The altars we build are made from our words and fueled by our actions. Will we burn sacrifices to our idols at these altars, or will we destroy the idols themselves? If we burn them, we can begin to consecrate our lives to God.

In "A Time of Altars," Jack Hayford writes, "There is a place of 'altaring' and a price of altering. Altars have a price—God intends that something be 'altered' in us when we come to altars."[6] I don't believe that's for the worst, but for the better.

Such is the cost of seeing our lives transformed.

Much Afraid, Gideon, and us all share a commonality: a testing ground where we can examine the most cherished aspects of our lives. Be assured that we don't have to enter this with trepidation, or even unrest.

We can begin with a question:

Where is the peace of God leading you?

Before Gideon receives the instructions to tear down the altar to Baal and burn the Asherah pole, he encounters the angel of the Lord. He sees the Lord face-to-face, and it changes him. And in honor of that meeting, he builds his first altar and names it "The LORD Is Peace."

Peace alters us.

This name, *Yahweh Shalom*, does not indicate that there will be a change in the problems around us, but it does promise that there will be a fullness and a lack of strife within us. *Shalom* means "wholeness" and "completeness." It means "welfare" and "safety." The Lord Is Peace points us to the one who does not leave us empty, but who delivers. When our needs are satisfied, and when they are met, there is no longer a reason to serve an idol.

Another question you might ask is this: Where is the fullness of God leading you?

If you desire no other thing, then you won't bend yourself to compromise for lesser things. For example, if the approval of others can't satiate you, then you won't make decisions based on it.

We won't be filled up by counterfeit idols, but we can by God's peace and presence. In God's presence, we are provided for. The *shalom* of the Lord is available to us, at this moment.

We can leave behind what's been harming us without looking back. We can say what needs to be said without fear of retribution. We don't have to perform or conform for the sake of recognition or even, acceptance.

I have a rotating series of sticky notes and index cards that I tape to our full-length mirror in our bedroom. On it, I write out Scriptures, quotes, and reminders—things I'm working on believing and walking out in my life. There's one I've meditated on a lot lately that both challenges and delights me. It points to what the peace of God is leading me to: the hardest change I've had to make in the face of my idols, what many call the "fear of man."

The note says, "I will accept the discomfort that comes from being fully myself."[7]

It doesn't feel natural, but it's because it requires God's hand to make possible.

Discomfort outside of me. Peace within me.

I don't have to bow down to the expectations of others. I don't have to do what's wrong to be seen as right. I don't have to fit into anyone's mold to keep the peace because peace is already kept by the Lord.

Our hearts, like frustrating puzzles, have missing pieces. We spend so much of our life attempting to complete them. We push jagged-edged bits into those empty spots, hoping they'll heal us when they only end up hurting us. Fragmented, small, and based on merit, they cut us up from the inside.

But as Steffany Gretzinger sings to Jesus, "You don't give your heart in pieces."[8] He leaves his heart, or rather the Spirit, who carries peace with him. He says, "Peace I leave with you; my peace I give you. I do not give to you as the world gives. Do not let your hearts be troubled and do not be afraid" (John 14:27).

When Jesus left, he didn't leave us without support. He left us with someone. Making altars, burning idols, dismantling those things that can't and won't serve us—they're done in the power of the Spirit, with the Sprit's guidance, and with the Spirit's fruit.

The Holy Spirit empowers us to crucify our self-righteousness—turn it into dust. The Holy Spirit can't help but guide us into the truth that though we want to blame and condemn those people and circumstances that have hurt us, we too have been folded into that hurt. As hard as it may be to hear, we're responsible for our responses.

The Spirit of God doesn't just leave God's peace; the Spirit gives us freedom. As 2 Corinthians 3:17 affirms, "Now the Lord is the Spirit, and where the Spirit of the Lord is, there is freedom."

When we surrender ourselves and our lives to him, when we fear him more than others, we are resurrected from the ashes of our will and become more like Christ instead.

Gideon tears down his father's idols. Then he's filled with the Spirit. Afterward, the Lord leads him to victory. He overcomes the enemy. He doesn't lead an army of 32,000 on his side, but only 300. He doesn't win the battle with axes and spears, but with torches inside empty pitchers and with trumpets. When given the word, Gideon's men broke the pitchers to shine the light inside and sounded the trumpets. Together they stood their ground, and the army of 135,000 men fled.

Even while weak, we flex the Lord's strength in our obedience. We may never face 135,000 men, but the contempt of just one person may feel the same. When we're excluded, left out, and made to feel less than, we might feel as if we're being trampled by an army; their judgment may pierce us like spears.

But with the Spirit, we can overcome. We can live confidently.

We're reminded in Galatians 5:1, "It is for freedom that Christ has set us free. Stand firm, then, and do not let yourselves be burdened again by a yoke of slavery."

Once we've destroyed these idols, may we never permit them in our lives again.

With peace, I took a break from church, and with peace I returned. I no longer overcompensate. I turn down what I need to without guilt. I am who I am without pretense. I don't hold back. I can be a part of the body of Christ because of who Christ is.

We can be led into this life, not in fear of rejection, but in the safety of Christ's love. We can live at peace with ourselves even when someone turns their back on us. We can come without our weapons to those who accuse us and reject us, fully believing that the Lord's voice and authority forms, guides, and protects us.

We are free from the death of rejection because we have dismantled the power of those who rejected us. We choose the Lord as our Savior.

PART TWO

. . . TO LIFE

INHALE

Lord, you are at home in my heart.

EXHALE

I am settled and safe in your love.

BASED ON EPHESIANS 3:17

CHAPTER 6

IN GOOD COMPANY

With full bellies after the Last Supper, the disciples of Jesus watched with curiosity as their Lord stripped himself of his clothes and tied a towel around his waist. Their confusion grew as he poured water into a basin. Then he began to dip their feet one by one into the basin and wash them.

At that point, he knew his death was near. He knew who would betray him. Yet out of the depths of his compassion for his friends, he humbled himself to serve them. He disrupted tradition in order to love them.

They had spent three and a half years in likeminded pursuit of God, traveling, sharing meals, and working all day together. I imagine they prayed for each other, laughed, and plumbed the depths of their hearts. After washing their feet, Jesus demonstrated this closeness by pronouncing them his friends. He used the word *friend*, or *philos* in Greek, which also means "beloved." Jesus had a deep affection for each of these men and didn't use this designation flippantly. He chose it as a term of endearment, an emotional expression dripping with intimacy. He cherished his disciples.

Jesus's friendship with them was not unlike the friendships we have with one another.

The first time I saw my two former best friends after our friendships had ended, they were together at our local library. On that random Friday, I had taken my kids to stockpile stacks of books for the weekend. Out of the peripheral of my eyes, I could see their kids bobbing along the bookshelves looking for something to read. I knew that it wouldn't be long before they saw me. I felt a surge of adrenaline pump through my body, and my heart began to beat faster. I felt afraid. I wanted to grab my kids and run. I didn't want to face the reality of what our friendships had become. I wanted to pretend I was okay, but I wasn't.

At that moment, my youngest grabbed my hand and led me across the room to a hidden corner. Glory and Nash joined us, and I began to read to my kids, focusing my attention on every word. Inwardly, I was in shambles. I hoped that I could avoid the awkwardness of talking with them.

I didn't. We spoke. Amid the small talk, I tried to get ahold of myself. Somehow, my heart had made its way into my throat. I tried to swallow back the bitter taste of loneliness and sadness. I tried to hide the tears that formed in the corners of my eyes. I felt so angry at how they had chosen each other but had left me behind.

We'd built our lives together. We had our babies and raised them together, celebrated holidays and birthdays together, and even helped each other move into our homes. For years, not a day would go by without a text message, a voice text, or a playdate. It seemed like we'd be friends forever and like we were all headed in the same direction.

Truth was, this had been the first and only time I had ever felt so close to someone other than my husband. For most of my life, I struggled to befriend other women. I couldn't seem to create or maintain friendships with them. I always felt a little different; maybe a little too hard to understand. But with these two, I finally felt seen and deeply cared for. Not only did we have fun together, but we could have meaningful conversations.

These weren't unbalanced relationships, with one giving more than the others; there was mutuality. We encouraged and supported one another. We were honest. I didn't have to be anyone other than myself.

It was a gift—to discover people who truly welcomed me as I was.

Which made it all the more difficult when it ended.

I feel this specific hardship is best summed up by an anonymous quote my grandmother kept in one of her journals. It said, "To lose a friend in whom one had invested something of one's personality was, I discovered, to have lost a certain amount of one's self."

No one prepares you for the grief that comes from losing a friend. It's quite unlike anything else I've ever experienced. It would take me a long time to recover from it.

The end began with a simple text. One of my friends

asked for space. It wasn't clear why she needed it or what had caused her to set such a boundary. She didn't want to talk; she wanted time to think. Concerned, we gave her what she asked for. One week turned into a few; then a few turned into a month. I didn't hear from her. Then, to my surprise, my friends reconciled without me. She restored *their* relationship, but not ours.

Three months went by when I finally received a letter in the mail.

I saved it to read later. I suspected that it did not hold glad tidings, and I was right. As I soaked in the bath that night, I read page after page of her large and loopy handwriting— attempting to explain that it wasn't me, it was her. She did not like who I reminded her of.

And as such, she could no longer be my friend.

I tried to understand why our friendship wasn't worth fighting for. What had I done wrong?

Every word rubbed open wounds I hadn't known were still healing.

This rejection reactivated every insecurity I had about myself. Though rejection isn't always personal, it can sure feel that way.

I held on to my other friend. I was thankful I still had her. Until I didn't anymore.

It didn't take long to lose her too.

She tried to maintain a friendship with both me and the friend I was estranged from, but it simply wasn't working. A rift formed instead. She didn't want to have to choose between us. I believed she already had. It was corrosive. It dissolved our trust and challenged our loyalty to each other.

Suddenly I was suspicious of every one of her attempts to be a friend. I felt like she was faking, and as the distance between us grew, I decided that I'd had enough. I didn't want to get hurt, so I decided to take matters into my own hands.

I would end our friendship first.

Where our friendship once had been, a massive hole was left. The emptiness was heavy and impossible to ignore. I couldn't shake the memories. I couldn't ignore the loneliness. For some time, it felt like I would never recover.

Everywhere I turned, I remembered the fun we had together.

I had given my all to both women. When they were gone, it felt like a part of me was gone too. In many ways, I had come to define myself solely within the context of these relationships. And now I had to begin the difficult work of detangling my identity from them.

We are not defined by the absence of the people who didn't know how to love us.

Yet we will inevitably ask ourselves, "What's wrong with me?"

When you've been rejected, this question becomes a homily of despair. It's a bid for control. We think that if could figure out our problem, then maybe we could have prevented what was done to us. Sometimes that kind of thinking results in self-hatred and deeply rooted insecurity.

When others turn from you, it might seem like the only

thing you can do is turn away from yourself too. Rather than addressing what we may have *done* wrong (if anything), we decide that we *are* wrong. We let shame beat us up. Our inner critic grabs for the megaphone and hijacks our sense of self and our relationship to ourself.

In the absence of friends, loneliness doesn't have to be such a bad thing.

Sharon Hodde Miller summarized Henri Nouwen's thoughts in *The Wounded Healer* like this: "Loneliness is a gift—an opportunity to learn how to be at home with ourselves and Jesus."[1]

Loneliness can be an invitation to come home.

If I couldn't be seen and known by others, was I willing to at least see and know myself?

I dove back into the things that I loved. The pressure was off. I didn't have to conform or be something I wasn't. And I had the time. I learned to love being alone with my thoughts and rediscovered old hobbies I had ignored.

I felt content and at peace. I felt confident.

As I rebuilt my life, Jesus led me to a new friend I didn't expect: him.

Though I had known him as Savior, I hadn't quite turned to him the way I had turned to others. When I began to do so, I immediately noticed the difference.

Christ is always accessible, always advocating, and always assuring—he quieted the questions that I had about myself. He empowered me. He helped me to see that I got to choose what formed me—either shame or his friendship.

One is rife with criticism; the other abounds with compassion.

∽

Criticism is no friend of ours. Compassion, though, is a faithful companion.

Frederick Buechner describes compassion in *Wishful Thinking: A Seeker's ABC* like this: "Compassion is sometimes the fatal capacity for feeling what it is like to live inside somebody else's skin."[2] Compassion is, quite literally, to suffer with someone. We know Christ embodies this. His crucifixion is a reminder of how deep his empathy for us is. He did not simply imagine what we experience; he walked through it himself. He put himself in a flesh-covered body, mortal and vulnerable, and lived a human life.

Compassion is the hinge on which Jesus operates, swinging wide his open invitation to one and all. He knows what it feels like to live inside this skin.

Christ's response to us when we struggle with our mistakes, or even our value, sounds a lot less like condemnation and more like life:

> For he chose us in him before the creation of the world to be holy and blameless in his sight. (Eph. 1:4)

> For we are God's handiwork, created in Christ Jesus to do good works, which God prepared in advance for us to do. (Eph. 2:10)

Instead of putting our worth in our hands or the hands of others, we can allow Christ to determine it for us. He gives us permission to believe that we are not projects to be fixed, but souls to be loved. He calls us good.

Rejection, on the other hand, whispers that we'll never be enough. So we let it become fuel—driving us to achieve or accomplish more. We might say, "I'll prove you wrong," or "I'll show you what you're missing out on." We might seek revenge to inflict pain on the ones who have hurt us. But in the end, we only end up hurting ourselves.

Enough will never be sustainable.

Just as Icarus flew too close to the sun, we also might try to climb the heights of our potential—just to feel that we belong, to feel that we are worthy to be loved.

But we can't manage this.

As the tale goes, Icarus's father, Daedalus, fashioned wings made from leather that he attached feathers to with beeswax. Icarus and Daedalus were imprisoned by a king on the island of Crete and were desperate to escape. Daedalus warned his son to be careful as he flew—not to hover too low or fly too high. But Icarus ignored Daedalus and soared toward the heat of the sun, which melted the beeswax that held the feathers in place.

Icarus fell from the sky and plunged into the sea. His quest to climb higher and higher was his undoing, and it could be ours too if we're not careful.

There will always be more we want to do and people we want to prove ourselves to. Even if we succeed, we still won't be content.

When our esteem is contingent on outside circumstances or the varying opinions of others, we're destined to fall like Icarus did.

There is another way. We can move through rejection without criticism.

We can escape self-hatred with compassion.

Kristen Neff, pioneer and researcher of self-compassion, gives us a practical framework for exercising compassion toward ourselves—which aligns beautifully with the gospel. According to Neff, self-compassion is made up of three significant elements: self-kindness, common humanity, and mindfulness.[3]

In the context of rejection:

SELF-KINDNESS looks like giving ourselves grace and learning to be gentle with ourselves. We don't have to beat up ourselves over the hardships we've experience or the mistakes we make. In fact, we can learn to talk to ourselves like a friend and offer ourselves the same care.

COMMON HUMANITY is knowing we're not the only ones who have experienced rejection. We have all, in one way or another, experienced it. We are not alone. We're reminded that like us, others can relate to and connect with our stories. In many ways, this strengthens us. Others have gone before us in living through rejection, and others will follow too.

MINDFULNESS is the ability to see our feelings in a nonjudgmental and balanced way. We can acknowledge our emotions without seeing them as a weakness or without exaggerating them. We are willing to name them without fear or hesitation, but not let them govern our actions without our consent.

When we walk through each of these components and apply them to our lives, we naturally begin to tend to our needs—just as compassion compelled God to move toward us, self-compassion will drive us to be attentive to ourselves. We change because it's what is best for us instead of because we feel we are worthless.

How might I be as compassionate and gracious to myself as Christ has been to me?

We cannot argue that the Lord does not operate from compassion. We see it plainly in the Scriptures when it says, "The LORD is gracious and compassionate, slow to anger and rich in love. The LORD is good to all; he has compassion on all he has made" (Ps. 145:8–9).

How might I abound in love toward my humanity and be slow to anger toward myself in my failings? How might I be good to the whole of who I am instead of just the parts I deem worthy?

Sometimes we can be surprised at just how self-deprecating we are.

Would we say the same things we say to ourselves to someone we love?

It takes intention, but we can capture these thoughts and disciple them to be more considerate. One way to do this is to list the ones you have about yourself—the ones that are unkind—and write them down. You might write something like:

I am not worth fighting for.

or

No one is *for* me. Everyone is *against* me.

It hurts to know that at one time we may have or the other believed these to be true about ourselves. It's astonishing how unkind we can be.

It helps to know they came from a place that was hurt, broken, and desperate for mercy, and for someone to take our hand and say, "I see you."

We can give ourselves that mercy.

With prayer, contend with these thoughts. It might even be helpful to acknowledge what each thought might be implying you need. For example, if I think I'm not worth fighting for, that might mean that I desire to have an advocate. I want someone to want me and to protect me.

Then imagine what a friend might say to you if you shared these things with them. How would they encourage you? Write this down beside the unkind thought about yourself.

Imagine what Christ might say. Is there a specific Scripture that soothes and speaks truth to that thought?

What better way to replace our unkindness than with Christ's loving-kindness?

I might respond to these thoughts like this:

The LORD will fight for you; you need only to be still. (Ex. 14:14)

117

and

The LORD your God is with you, the Mighty Warrior who saves. He will take great delight in you; in his love he will no longer rebuke you, but will rejoice over you with singing. (Zeph. 3:17)

Start with one verse. When you're ready, add another. When you're done, put it somewhere where you can memorize it and absorb it.

When you find yourself spiraling into despair and discouragement, use it. In this way, "as God's chosen people, holy and dearly loved, clothe yourselves with compassion, kindness, humility, gentleness and patience. Bear with each other and forgive one another if any of you has a grievance against someone. Forgive as the Lord forgave you. And over all these virtues put on love, which binds them all together in perfect unity" (Col. 3:12–14).

We are not exempt from treating *ourselves* in the way Christ calls us to treat others.

You might want it to be harder than this, but you don't have to pay a price for kindness. It costs you nothing to receive what Christ paid dearly for.

What we might not be able to grasp with our minds, our bodies know all too well. Our bodies respond not just to external threats but to internal ones too. Self-criticism is a threat.

Like other threats, self-criticism activates our sympathetic nervous system, which is what hosts our fight, flight, or freeze response. Our nervous system is essential to our well-being. It controls everything from our thoughts and feelings to our muscles, senses, breathing, and heartbeat. When our sympathetic nervous system is in operation, it is trying to support us in surviving perceived danger. Our heart beats faster. Our muscles tense. Our pupils dilate. We become more agitated. Meanwhile, our systems are being flooded with cortisol and adrenaline—with stress. Naturally, I think it would be difficult to try to make a levelheaded decision about a relationship, a circumstance, or even oneself when you are in this state.

Self-criticism directs our attention to our deficiencies so that we can hustle to compensate.

It might even freeze us in despair.

I tend to be overwhelmed by my weakness. I focus on what I feel unqualified to do and thus am tormented by the fear of rejection and failure. Instantly, everything becomes heavier. I can feel the pressure suffocating me. Under stress, I will instinctively chastise myself for what I should be able to do better.

Instead of meeting myself with compassion, I meet myself with disdain. It is self-flagellation loaded with guilt and shame.

It is my tendency and what I am—dare I say—most comfortable with. In spite of what I know to be true, I label myself as bad when Christ has already declared me good. I attempt to judge what he has already been measured. The verdict is in. Compassion is our sentence.

Compassion uncovers our shame, and it names us as we are: beloved.

Compassion covers us in Christ's love. In our bodies, it

surges through our veins by way of oxytocin; it soothes us.[4] Oxytocin, like endorphins and serotonin, is a hormone that produces and promotes positive feelings. It functions as a neurotransmitter in the brain, a messenger bringing the good news from one neuron to another.

Oxytocin acts like a volume control switch. It helps our brains make sense of what is happening around and to us. Oxytocin is what bonds a mother to her newborn child so that she can know her baby's needs and attend to them. From simple touch to positive interactions, oxytocin helps us feel grounded, safe, calm, and connected. It helps us to trust.

Compassion is no platitude. It is power. Its strength keeps us steady—it's strong enough to pick us up when we fall. It sits with us when it's all too much. It reminds us of our belovedness when we're not enough. It doesn't require that we are more than we are. It doesn't respond to our striving—just our hearts, as they are. It allows us to simply breathe and to let Christ do what it is he came to do.

Self-deprecation and self-criticism are reflections of believing that our opinion, or the opinions of others, are *more important* than the opinion of Christ.

Paul explores this truth in a letter he writes, saying, "I care very little if I am judged by you or by any human court; indeed, I do not even judge myself. My conscience is clear, but that does not make me innocent. It is the Lord who judges me" (1 Cor. 4:3–4).

Whom do you let get the final say?

In explaining Paul's choice of words to the Corinthians, Timothy Keller writes in *The Freedom of Self-Forgetfulness* that Paul "goes one step further: he will not even judge himself. It is as if he says, 'I don't care what you think—but I don't care what I think. I have a very low opinion of your opinion of me—but I have a very low opinion of my opinion of me.'"[5] Keller reminds us that though Christ calls us friend, we call him Lord. He always gets the last word.

Though I trashed it the same day I received and read it, the handwritten letter from my friend lived in my head. Every page mocked me; every excuse felt like an insult. I didn't want them to, but her words immortalized themselves in my head.

For a while there, I was a mess. And completely overwhelmed. Until I let the Lord in.

In Ephesians 3:16–17, Paul prays, "From his glorious, unlimited resources he will empower you with inner strength through his Spirit. Then Christ will make his home in your hearts as you trust in him. Your roots will grow down into God's love and keep you strong" (NLT).

When a true friend enters your home, you usually let down your guard. They might know where the cups are, navigating your kitchen with familiarity and ease. They see the mess and hardly glance at it. You've come to expect that they have compassion for you—grace for your fumbling, for your dirty sink, for the crumbs that you haven't swept up. They welcome you at your worst, and they celebrate you at your best. They don't live as spectators; they are involved. They've brought a plate of cookies over, and they're ready and willing to share.

What a picture of Jesus—lounging in the oversized chair in the living room, a friend to you—lending their presence and reminding you that you're loved.

⌒

In our home, we have a sign above the arch that welcomes our guests into our living room. It's small, but every letter is capitalized, shouting, "COME AS YOU ARE." I bought it without really appreciating its significance. I didn't yet realize that this is what it means to be a friend. I didn't yet understand what it means to have a friend in Jesus.

Unintentionally, I had kept him at arm's length. I don't think I really knew how to come as I was. How could he be more to me than Lord and Savior?

Was there room for my questions? Was there a place for my doubt?

Could I really stop pretending that life would always work out?

Then, one day, the dam broke. Thankfully, I was home alone—a rarity. I had just learned that someone I knew was getting something I had wanted for years. It wasn't something you could buy. It was a dream realized.

I felt anger flood my veins and immediately raised my hands in the air and slammed them on the kitchen counter. As my eyes welled up with tears and my throat filled with rage, I roared into the empty kitchen, "Why, Lord? Why do you forget me? Where are you?"

Months before, my therapist had asked me when the last time was that I'd had a completely unfiltered conversation with the Lord. At first, I countered her challenge with a reply of disbelief: "I'm nothing but honest." After thinking about it, I realized that just wasn't true. I had harbored a lot of thoughts: frustration with the injustice of losing relationships and discouragement over the way my past was still very much impacting my life. I felt like I carried the weight of the world and like God had done very little to restore what was shattered. I knew I had these expectations for what I wanted my life to look like and disappointment that it didn't.

I had been holding back. I persisted under false pretenses instead of sharing the truth. I didn't want Jesus to leave me. I thought I could fake it until I made it. I had been told that I was too much, so why would it be any different with the Lord?

When I finally expressed my distress and dismay, I realized Christ hadn't moved any farther from me than where I had put him myself. In fact, it was with my honesty and an open heart that for the first time I felt his loving presence.

We can get it wrong. We can think our friendship with Christ is contingent on us. But he chose us. He befriended us. He shows up for us. Even when we're a mess.

His faithfulness is part of who he is. Even when we're not faithful, he is. To be anything else would be to deny himself. His friendship wraps itself around us like a security blanket. Under his cover, we can show up as we are because he will never leave.

There's nothing like the feeling of revealing the truest and most vulnerable parts of yourself and being loved instead of scorned, held instead of rejected, pursued instead of abandoned, and favored instead of forgotten.

Christ doesn't just move toward us, pursuing us. He intercedes for us.

In a room we cannot yet inhabit, Jesus advocates for us and prays for us (Rom. 8:34). He gives us permission to ask for and to receive what we need.

We let his compassion for us inform the compassion we should have for ourselves and for others. We let it become the framework in which we can befriend ourselves—treating our bodies and souls as people to be loved, instead of hated and always pressed to be more.

The same feet Jesus washed at the Last Supper would run and hide, forsaking him when he was taken from the garden of Gethsemane. Judas would exchange his relationship with Jesus for mere coins and a moment of clout by leading a group of soldiers and officials to the garden to arrest Jesus. With a kiss on the cheek, Judas betrayed Jesus.

As Christ was hauled away, those he loved turned their backs on him—they scattered in fear for their safety. In agonizing succession, Peter denied knowing Jesus three times. The crowd chanted over Jesus, "Crucify him." He was spit at and mocked as he was beaten and battered before he was hung on the cross.

Christ walked hand in hand with rejection.

His own brothers struggled to believe that he was the Son of God. He was judged by people who questioned whether any good thing could come out of his hometown, Nazareth. Though many crowds followed him, they also deserted him.

The government could not tolerate him. The Pharisees and religious leaders constantly barraged him, too threatened by what he stood for to accept him. Then, when it mattered most, Pilate let the people have their way with him.

The pain of rejection in our lives echoes Jesus's.

We are marginalized for our upbringing, our appearance, and our personality. We are left behind because of our lack of skills or talent. We are overlooked because we live in a world that requires us to shrink and stay quiet and small. We are othered because we are in pain, because our lives aren't picture perfect, because we're in process, or because we challenge the status quo. We are estranged from our own flesh and blood when we don't agree or see eye to eye.

We are not alone. We can be certain that others have experienced these things. And we can be certain that Christ knows our suffering intimately.

His compassion for us isn't pity; it's understanding.

Compassion is no trope; it's not something that just makes us feel good.

It provokes personal and societal change.

Studies show that compassion protects against stress, anxiety, and depression. As compassion grows in us, it increases our empathy—it supports us in becoming more connected. It shifts our focus from self-centerenedness to selflessness.

The power of compassion doesn't end with us.

I am convinced that as we receive the kindness and friendship of Christ and learn to be kind to ourselves, in time we will know what it is to walk with someone and for them to walk alongside us too.

INHALE

I breathe.

EXHALE

You breathe life into me.

BASED ON GENESIS 2:7

CHAPTER 7

RITUALS OF HUMILITY

The tendons in the backs of my legs groan and buckle under the weight of my expectations. I can feel every ache of my body as I run on our cheap treadmill in our unfinished basement. Anxiety bubbles under the surface of each loud breath I take. *Is my body capable of this?* My arms feel heavy as I move them up and down. I feel weak. This task I signed myself up for seems impossible.

It's March. We're deep in the throes of a Colorado winter. Sometime at the advent of the New Year, I had decided this was the year I would run my first half-marathon—13.1 miles of just my body and me making amends for all the hurt we had caused each other. United once again. For good.

Over the last two years of Covid, I had gained the weight not just of the countless quiches I'd eaten but of a broken heart finally making its presence known. Its cries had gotten loud, pleading for me to take notice of its pain. But it had been too hard to listen, so—like with my phone and the spotty cell service in the forest near my home—we became disconnected.

Pride had blocked any attempts my body had made at reuniting with my heart and soul. If I spent too long paying attention to the undercurrent of belief that fed my anxiety, it would become too much. I found myself asking, *Am I not enough? Am I too much? Why do I always feel as if I am lacking?*

Rejection had made its mark on me, and instead of fighting it, I succumbed—my perspective of myself dwindling into regular plays of passive self-hatred. I didn't have much to hold on to in January. I was still reeling from losing my friends, and I felt lost all over again.

So many significant people had rejected me that I began to reject myself. And while I had done much work to heal, I began to hide under the idea that I was just fine on my own. *On my own*, I thought, *I can fully heal again.* There could be no tenderness there. Vulnerability wasn't allowed. I had to harden myself and make a way through this life avoiding the possibility of hurt. Oh, how could God make me so incomplete? So weak? I vowed never to feel such lack or disappointment again.

Yet this posture did nothing but usher in more of what overwhelmed me. Instead of taking the risk to see my life filled with goodness, I could only ever see emptiness.

I had limited the work God could do. I let him into only the parts of my healing I felt I could control or grasp. As long as I could come out looking like I had it all together, I would let God heal me. Somewhere in the trenches of my faith I thought this was what it looked like to be a good Christian.

I didn't realize I'd only ever known a disconnected faith, one that left my body out of the equation. I only let God into the parts of my life that had already been made complete, made perfect.

Rejection made me afraid to embody all that I was. But in resisting, I became more of a walking shadow than a light on a hill.

I had to lay it all down. I had to come to the end of myself to meet myself and to see God again—to live a faith embodied not just in my strength, but in my weakness too.

But how could I do this? You might be wondering the same thing.

It starts with not only admitting our fragility but *leaning into it.*

Jesus demonstrated the nature of humility in his life by his mere presence—his willingness to come to Earth and be one like us. But we also see it poignantly in the death of his friend Lazurus, a man whom Jesus loved.

Twice Jesus said to those who sent for him and to Mary who wept for her brother that Lazurus would not stay dead. For God's glory, Lazurus would rise to live once again. Although Christ had the confidence of one who knew the plans of God, he was moved by Mary's grief at her brother's tomb.

Jesus wept.

These two words convey the heart of the Man of Sorrows, well acquainted with suffering, unafraid to feel the weakness of the mortal human body, its bounded and limited life, and aware of how quickly this life can be taken. Spurgeon taught, "He wept to baptize our prayers unto God." He wept to show us that we can do the same.[1]

Christ instructs us in how we can live in this finite world. Though we know death is not the end for us, we can still be attuned and present to the groans and aches this world compels in us. Jesus was not ashamed of his humanity, and neither should we be. In fact, it's in our humanity that we find our humility.

Our tears reflect this. We offer our weeping in surrender and trust that Christ meets us in the valleys just as he carries us to the mountaintops.

We so easily spurn our weakness, compartmentalizing our pain and our lack. From this pride, we speak in platitudes. We convince ourselves that rejection doesn't hurt. We pretend that we're content with being redirected elsewhere. We declare that something else will come along. We are desperate to prove ourselves and to prove God. Yet even God's Son did not hurry to do so. Jesus had no need to defend his Father by policing Mary or his grief. His tears did not minimize God's glory. And neither do ours.

Humility is not so much a reflection of what we can or cannot do as it is a signpost pointing to our belief in what God can and will do in and through us. Humility is putting God in his rightful place: above us. It is our view of ourselves filtered through the kingdom.

Thus, humility does not require hiding.

$$\sim$$

Three months after I started my training, that painful mile I could hardly finish in the beginning had stretched into three, then six, and then ten. I laugh at the ease with which I tackled the distance. Still the first few miles stayed the hardest. My body takes it time to warm up to the idea of moving. It questions my desire, challenging me to quit before I find my pace. But eventually I fall into a sweet rhythm as I trace the path by my house once more, every stride with less pageantry and more memorial.

This trail has become holy. Even though we live in a city, the patch of forest near my home remains mostly underdeveloped. Houses are scattered throughout, but the path through the pine trees where I run still feels remote and wild. As I'm engulfed by trees, the silence is punctuated only by the leaves and needles quaking in the wind. At a couple of points, if you stop and look in the right direction, you can see Pikes Peak rise 14,115 feet in elevation, its snowcapped point a beacon of majesty. It reminds me of our anchor, God. It's here where I feel him the most, where I often feel the most like myself.

Running has become more ritual than labor. My efforts are more humble than vain. Every breath is a prayer, every heartbeat an extension of the God who created me, a reminder of my mortality. I can't make my heart beat any better than it already does or force my breaths to last longer than they should. When life becomes too much, I'm fully aware of how much I think I can't, and how every time I reveal my weakness, God covers it with the presence of Christ telling me I can. I'm aware, here, of the mercy I'm given daily.

How often do we allow ourselves to live in vulnerability?

In the spaces where we feel the most unsure, uncomfortable, or unequipped? In the places where we're afraid we'll be hurt the most? Where the possibility of disappointment lingers more tangibly than we'd like? Or where we're certain we'll be turned away and dismissed?

Humility allows us to forge new paths. Its fruit is healing—in us and through us.

Many of us have misconceptions about humility. For our purposes, humility is the practice of recognizing that God's way is better than our own. It means recognizing our absolute need for him. It is a gift to us because it allows us to receive God's grace.

In the hands of God's grace, we're able to love ourselves and learn to love others.

Running has been my guide back to this grace.

Much of what we experience is remembered in our bodies. The neglect, the abandonment, and the disregard become etched into our bones. Whether we acknowledge it or not, our bodies tell our stories. But they also try to write them too. As a therapist, I see this often. What compels someone to seek help isn't only that they're frustrated with what's going on in their lives; they're also imprisoned by what's happening in their bodies. We often want to be treated for one or the other, forgetting that they work together.

Many clients get to the point where aspects of their life become too heavy to hold. For others, these realities are too hard to acknowledge. It's terrifying to attend to these parts of ourselves or, as they say, "to feel our feelings."

Every time I tied my shoes and set my watch for a run, a gallery of thoughts, desperate to be heard and attended to, rose up in my mind. I couldn't believe I'd actually registered for the half-marathon. Didn't I know the only result would be failure? These thoughts mocked the hope that had begun to give spring to my step. My past trumpeted the lie that I would never be enough to be loved, to be embraced as I am. These thoughts were heavy and overwhelming.

Running allowed me to tend to the damage rejection had done in me.

I would struggle to breathe. I'd feel my heartbeat quicken, and at times I began to panic, thinking I'd die before I could take another step. But instead of moving away from the pain, I ran into it. I didn't deny my weakness. Instead, I learned to embrace it.

When we move our bodies, we move our brains. We can learn new patterns that result in the restoration of our minds and souls. In fact, when we show our bodies that they can move through discomfort and still be safe, that experience restores us—it strengthens us for what is to come. When we allow ourselves space to be weak, we learn to embody the belief that God makes us strong.

Exercise is one of the best and most efficient ways to increase neurogenesis, which is what creates brand-new neurons in our brains.[2] Specifically, exercise stimulates the neurons in our hippocampus, the part of our brain that plays a major role in our learning and memory.

We practice what we want to believe.

By running, I learned that I was safe in the hands of God. This was the story I wanted my body to know.

But running wasn't the primary factor in my healing. It was just a conduit for other rituals of humility. It was a reminder that I desperately needed to practice lament, petition, and praise—that there were other ways to fellowship with God.

We can't know what we need until we need it, so I hadn't practiced some of these rituals of humility in quite some time. They hadn't become disciplines.

Certain disciplines might come more easily to us than others. But all are necessary in our path toward God and toward healing and in our spiritual formation. These tools shouldn't be reserved only for times of crisis but should play a role in our everyday faith.

These acts of humility allow us to re-posture our hearts toward Christ, to remember what brought us to him, and to give him room in our lives.

LAMENT

Along with our desire to be strong, many of us have a persistent desire to remain positive. Yet we confuse positivity with hope. We believe that to have hope we must always look on the bright side. At times, we might believe that optimism seems more pious. We forget to lament.

God isn't looking to form us into robots that are unable to compute the brokenness, nuance, and tension we live in every day. Lament reflects our willingness to look at the real suffering that happens in and around us, to know that God meets us in it.

Jesus wept. He saw the irrefutable reality of our human bodies and grieved it.

How can we know the depths of our desperation if we haven't plumbed them?

Lament isn't for the self-righteous; it is for the faithful.

We know that Christ can hold what we can't bear.

Years ago, when Ethan and I made the choice to have a baby, we thought, like most parents, that making a baby would be the easiest part of the process. Months passed as I kept expecting to see both lines on the pregnancy test. I'd peer into the indicator window willing myself to see what wasn't there—buying more tests than was necessary, thinking that *this* time would be different.

Then, one day, the lines were there—bold, dark, and telling. I was pregnant.

As the weeks went by, I tried to keep our delight a secret. I imagined the day when I would hold our child in my arms. I spent each day planning every detail of the nursery and bought the cutest clothes. I felt special, harboring this joy in my heart that no one knew about but us.

We couldn't keep it secret. Ethan would run into the local Walgreens and sheepishly get back into the car, telling me he had told the cashier—a stranger—everything. Even though we had made an agreement to wait, it wasn't long before the staff at the church knew, as did my closest colleagues on the administration team at the elementary school where I was a school counselor.

It was there, in between classroom lessons and small groups that I realized something was terribly wrong.

I stood in the staff bathroom, panicking while dialing the ob-gyn to talk with someone about what was happening. The nurse who took my call reassured me that bleeding was normal at this stage of the pregnancy. She told me just to hang in there. So I did. I pretended that everything was fine. Maybe positive thoughts would save me.

It wasn't, and they didn't.

Later that night, I ended up in the emergency room. I was miscarrying, and it had taken a turn for the worse. I needed surgery, and they prepared to get me in as soon as they could.

They left us in what felt like the coldest room in the hospital. Its walls were empty, and besides a small chair and the hospital bed, nothing else was in it. I writhed in torment as we waited for hours to see the doctor. I was shivering, and I begged the staff to bring me as many of their impossibly thin blankets as they had.

As the reality of what we were facing hit me like a wave, tears streamed down my face. I was grieving for what was and what could have been.

Ethan grabbed my Bible out of my bag, and I asked him to read something to me—anything. He stumbled and struggled through various Scriptures, trying to process through his own grief.

In this barren room, and with my soon-to-be barren womb, I felt for the first time the tangible presence of God. I can't explain it. But I knew he was there, hovering over us.

Lament shapes us. It shapes our faith.

It names our humanity. Our need. Our desperation. Our mess.

It tells of our inability to predict the future and to protect ourselves from it.

It shares in our confusion, discouragement, and questions.

Lament does not hide us from God. It pushes us toward him, and God toward us.

Ethan turned to Psalm 139 and read, "Even the darkness will not be dark to you; the night will shine like the day, for darkness is as light to you" (v. 12).

Though I had heard these words before, they suddenly came alive. God would meet us in this darkness. I didn't have to find the bright side because God himself was the light.

We may feel overwhelmed, cast down, fraught with fear and despair, but God sees right through it all. We try desperately to make meaning out of that which we cannot see clearly—this ever-present dark in difficult times. But God, as the light bearer, illuminates the darkness.

Lament invites us to focus less on trying to understand what could be happening to us and more on who will walk alongside us. God knows the way through, and that gives us the freedom to just trust, and be.

PETITION

Like lament, petition asks us to be vulnerable and willing to ask for what we need. We fear this, because at times we're afraid of what could live at the end of the ask. Mainly, we don't want to be told no.

So we pray, but we pray timidly. We pray with mistrust. We self-protect even as we approach our protector.

And to be honest, we overcomplicate this process by emphasizing the formality of the act instead of leaning into the intimacy. God doesn't want to have a business meeting; he wants to have a conversation.

We may not always know what to say. Still, we have permission to show up, with arms open wide, our desperation a call to God. As Anne Lamont writes in *Help, Thanks, Wow: The Three Essential Prayers*, "Take a quavering breath and say, 'Help.' . . . It is the hardest prayer, because you have to admit defeat—you have to surrender, which is the hardest thing any of us do, ever."[3]

Every silent tear, every sob, every groan is translated for us. The Spirit intercedes to bring our prayers to God. And Jesus himself advocates for us.

Petitions are also a call for deliverance—often from ourselves.

Whether we understand it or not, our Father will provide for us. Jesus reiterates this in Matthew 7:9–11 when he says, "Which of you, if your son asks for bread, will give him a stone? Or if he asks for a fish, will give him a snake? If you, then, though you are evil, know how to give good gifts to your children, how much more will your Father in heaven give good gifts to those who ask him!"

His good gift is himself.

God responds. Maybe with provision, the way we hope, or in the least expected of ways—but always, we can trust, with the Lord's presence.

I have found particular comfort in the petitions found in the Litany of Humility attributed to Cardinal Rafael Merry del Val, the secretary of state to Pope Pius X in the early 1900s:

O Jesus, meek and humble of heart, hear me.
From the desire of being esteemed, deliver me, Jesus.
From the desire of being loved, deliver me, Jesus.
From the desire of being extolled, deliver me, Jesus.
From the desire of being honored, deliver me, Jesus.
From the desire of being praised, deliver me, Jesus.
From the desire of being preferred to others, deliver
     me, Jesus.
From the desire of being consulted, deliver me, Jesus.
From the desire of being approved, deliver me, Jesus.
From the fear of being humiliated, deliver me, Jesus.
From the fear of being despised, deliver me, Jesus.
From the fear of suffering rebukes, deliver me, Jesus.
From the fear of being calumniated, deliver
     me, Jesus.
From the fear of being forgotten, deliver me, Jesus.
From the fear of being ridiculed, deliver me, Jesus.
From the fear of being wronged, deliver me, Jesus.
From the fear of being suspected, deliver me, Jesus.
That others may be loved more than I, Jesus, grant
     me the grace to desire it.
That others may be esteemed more than I, Jesus,
     grant me the grace to desire it.
That, in the opinion of the world, others may
     increase and I may decrease, Jesus, grant me
     the grace to desire it.
That others may be chosen and I set aside, Jesus,
     grant me the grace to desire it.
That others may be praised and I unnoticed, Jesus,
     grant me the grace to desire it.

> That others may be preferred to me in everything,
>   Jesus, grant me the grace to desire it.
> That others may become holier than I, provided
>   that I may
> become as holy as I should, Jesus, grant me the
>   grace to desire it.[4]

When we petition for deliverance and for help, we're asking for freedom from that which troubles us.

In both lament and petition, we hesitate to present our whole selves in fear of being denied. We're afraid to ask too much, want too much, and be too human. I can't help but wonder, if we can't be our whole selves with God, who can we be our whole selves with? In these cases, humility isn't an act of self-denial but of discovering who we are in God and with God.

We can't scare God away. Even at our worst, and most needy.

In the same way we train our bodies as we move them in and out of discomfort, we do the same with our hearts when we practice sitting in lament and petition. It prepares us.

PRAISE

As I ran mile after mile in preparation for the looming race, I found myself coming as I was. When I processed heavy burdens and life complaints, I sometimes broke down in tears, but other times every step was a silent petition before the Lord. I'd stand in the shadow of the trees wanting to be more than just a shadow of myself. I'd hold every fragment up to the light, surrendering it to God.

Eventually, it wasn't only lament and petition that escaped my mouth—I started praising him too. I've found that inevitably, the former will naturally evolve into the latter, without coercion or obligation. It's another reminder that we don't have to fear lament and petition because they'll always point us to Christ.

I come from a seemingly dispassionate faith tradition, so when I met my husband and attended his church for the very first time, I was blown away by their charisma. *Terrified* would probably be a better way to describe it.

During worship, people went to kneel at the front in droves, not because they were asked to, but because they wanted to. They raised their hands and danced and sang with every measure of their voices. I wanted what they had. I wanted the courage to forget myself; to let go of my inhibitions.

While there are a variety of ways to worship, I knew I wanted to praise uninhibited. It took me years to move my arms from my sides to above my head. It only felt right to give all of myself with not just my voice, but my actions too.

Like lament and petition, surrender is vital to our praise. We forget what's happening around us with others and focus more on what has happened and is happening with us and God.

When we're released from thinking so much about ourselves, it gives us the freedom to run. It grants us the freedom to sprint toward hope.

Praise is the ultimate act of humility. It's not as simple

as forgetting ourselves. It is also inhabiting the truth of who God is in our lives. It requires us to look for hope despite disappointment or discouragement.

Praise is our declaration that we really do believe God's way is better. Praise is shouting into the dark that God's greatest gift to us is himself.

I often think of what was said of David's worship: "David was dancing before the LORD with all his might" (2 Sam. 6:14). David said to another who despised his actions, "I will become even more undignified than this, and I will be humiliated in my own eyes" (2 Sam. 6:22). He didn't act like one who was despised, disdained, and rejected, but like one who had been chosen, anointed, and loved by God.

Praise can't live in tandem with pride. Neither can lament or petition.

David couldn't help himself. The revelation of the Lord in his life and all God had done became embodied in his response. So it can be with us.

Praise and worship are melodies of sacrifice. The author of Hebrews 13:15 writes, "Through Jesus, therefore, let us continually offer to God a sacrifice of praise—the fruit of lips that openly profess his name." Praise costs us. We may not know what is to come. We may never know. Still, we let ourselves sit in the mystery of it all and exalt the Lord anyway.

When we're able to walk into the room that we most want filled in our life—a room that signifies our deepest desire but is the emptiest, the most desolate, maybe even the most disappointing—and still celebrate, honor, and give thanks to God, that requires our all.

As with humility, you can never truly "arrive" when you're a runner. Once the 5k or half-marathon is over, you're already thinking about the next race. You're trying to quicken your pace or run even more miles. That's why running, for me anyway, is never about the time or the medal, but the ritual, the engrained habit of day after day, lacing up my shoes, grabbing my sunglasses, and heading out the door. I'll run the same routes repeatedly, and I'll listen to the same playlist, sometimes the same song.

As much as I love it, I hate it. It doesn't matter how often I run—it's still hard to get started. I don't want to do it, somedays. Those days, I'm reminded so much of my weakness. The treadmill is the worst of all. There's nothing like three miles of literally facing a wall to force you to face yourself and what you think you're capable of.

Still, I can show up mad, elated, or even sad, and every step will meet me where I am. There's no competition here, no need to pretend to be something I'm not, when all that I need is to press in and on.

Humility asks the same of us where pride requires us to posture and pretend. We're open in humility. In pride, we're stubborn and unrelenting, and what's stuck within us stays stuck.

What would it look like to embody humility? To let it be a part of who we are? Not as something to strive toward, but as something to pick up and put on every single day.

We desperately need to be reminded of our weakness and dependence. But how?

I set several alarms on my phone to help me be mindful of my need.

I set these alarms in the form of several questions. Early in the morning, the first catches my attention and asks,

Could you let God protect you?

Then again, later in the afternoon:

Where are you at in trusting Jesus with this?

I don't feel so much conviction as permission to be human. It's okay to be human, to feel angry or sad or tender. We know we have these needs—but are we willing to let God have them?

Humility is a gateway to God's grace.

The more we allow ourselves to be more human, the more we can make space for others to be human too. We learn that when we lean into our dependence, we become not weaker, but stronger.

The beauty in being transformed from the inside out is that we can't help but impact those around us. It draws us closer to God and others closer to us. It allows us to be soft when rejection demands that we remain hard. Where rejection creates division, humility unashamedly declares, "I won't give up on you."

Humility is not an act of defeat. Humility reminds us that we are not at war with what we see, but with what is unseen. We do not have to be in competition with others, or even ourselves.

Our lives are more than our reputations, others' perceptions, or our accomplishments. We can't perform into God's love when it has already been poured out on us.

Humility is deciding that we don't have to hide ourselves any longer from the gaze of God. We yield to his love. It's also an understanding that because we're accepted by him, we no longer have to hide from others either.

Outside of relationships and connection, it means that we can finally take that risk we've been avoiding. We can take the leap. We can run hard after our dreams. We can try and try again, even as we meet failure after failure.

Humility is, ultimately, to surrender.

When we look at the root of this word, *surrender*, we see that in the Old French it means "to give up and to hand over." When we lament, when we ask for help, when we give praise, we are in each one handing our lives over to Christ.

Our tears. Our fears. Our hope. Our anticipation. Our needs. We give them up.

We can live open-handed, knowing we won't ever live empty-handed.

As we round the corner, I can see the inflatable finish line banner above the horizon. This is it. I am nearly done running 13.1 miles, and the remaining part of the course is all uphill. It is almost 80 degrees outside, and I am covered in sweat. My body can't cool down, my heart rate can't come down, and I feel a strange mix of exhaustion and elation.

I can hear my husband and kids cheering, "Go, Mom, go!"

My friend takes my hand, and we look toward the finish line with anticipation.

I've run over 300 miles in six months. The shoes I bought in January have dulled and turned gray over time from dirt trails, snow-covered roads, and dirty treadmills. They, like my faith, have been broken in. Stretched. Brought through all sorts of new territory. I ran when I didn't want to. I ran when I felt like I could. I ran when I wanted nothing more than to give up. I ran when I needed to cry. I ran when I wanted to dance. I ran when I felt despair. I ran when all was right with the world.

Lament. Petition. Praise.

Every stride forward is evidence of these new rhythms—my desperate need on display.

This is my newfound rhythm of humility, of asking for and receiving grace for myself and my circumstances. This is what will allow me to move beyond myself into healing—to become someone who lives wholeheartedly with open hands even in front of those who might deny or reject me.

As we cross the finish line, I raise my arms in celebration.

I can just breathe knowing my life is in God's hands.

INHALE

You take what's empty and fill it full.

EXHALE

You satisfy the longings of my soul.

BASED ON PSALM 107:9

CHAPTER 8

LOSE YOURSELF

When we are really able to see ourselves, we are able to see Christ all the more. There's no pomp or circumstance, just a simple acknowledgment of our need and our humanity. Our weakness instructs us in humility. It opens our hearts to encounters with Christ that our pride would otherwise hinder.

Humility leads us to him, and it also moves us toward others. It cultivates empathy. With humility comes the recognition that no one is exempt from Christ's love—not us or the people who have hurt us. We begin to embody the truth that we can love because he first loved us. It moves us from an egocentric worldview to a more altruistic mindset. The Messiah—who embraces us so fully, so wholly—inspires us to be someone who gives because he can, someone who wishes to take others by the hand to introduce them to him, to live in utter abandon because of how beloved we are and how holy he is.

It is a revelation. What Christ does for us, he also does for others. Often by using us.

Though I have followed Christ for more than half my life, for some time I felt confused about my place and role within the church. I grew up among formidable women who let nothing hold them back from pursuing the lives they hoped for and who felt the freedom to be who they were created to be. But I also felt the tension between what I knew and what it felt like I was allowed to be a part of the body of Christ. I often questioned how God really felt about me. When I read the Bible, I sometimes struggled to see myself within its pages. Then I met the woman at the well in John 4.

Like so many others, I used to read this story and misunderstand it—and misunderstand her. Wasn't she just another problem to be solved? Yet when we look carefully, we see that she was just someone to be loved. She encountered the goodness and grace of Jesus, and she was changed. What we often miss is that her changing *also* changed others.

The woman stumbles upon Jesus, and the encounter punctures deep into her soul. We find that Jesus will reveal himself to her as the Son of God, but first, Jesus reveals her to herself. In both, hope abounds and overflows. No one is ever the same. Excitement and freedom swell and expand so much within her that she cannot not keep them to herself.

As with the man at Bethesda, Jesus literally goes out of

his way to meet this woman. Instead of taking the long way around Samaria, a region Jews typically avoided, he travels directly into it. He's weary and alone. His disciples have gone off to grab lunch, leaving Jesus to rest on his own at the well as the sun shines high above him.

It's at this moment that the woman approaches the well with her water jug, desperate for a drink in more ways than one. She's not the only one who is thirsty. Jesus is too. He asks for a drink.

What's happening between the woman and Jesus is astounding. It's counter to their culture in every way. The woman is clearly caught off guard.

Who is she that he would be speaking to her?

First, she is a Samaritan. Second, she is a woman. She comes from the people the Jews detest. And at that time, women were considered second-class citizens. As Kristi McLelland teaches in *Jesus and Women*, "The Samaritan woman's testimony is considered unreliable and unworthy to listen to. She is to be seen but not heard."[1] She is not only a problem to be solved, but a voice to be silenced. Or so it might seem. The story that we tell about the woman is that she is an adulteress and a prostitute. But we simply don't have enough to judge her. We don't have any evidence of that.

We know that she has been married and divorced, possibly even widowed, five times and is now living with yet another man. Yet we cannot assume that she's put herself in this position by living immorally. It's likely that because of a lack of living male relatives, her only option has been to use marriage as a resource. Scripture doesn't tell us why she remarried, only that she did.

Like us, she did what she could to protect herself.

It was quite unusual that she came to draw water at midday. Typically, this chore was completed in the evening. We can't know for sure, but we might surmise that she had a complicated relationship with her community. She might have felt marginalized. She might have felt ostracized. Though she was not living alone, I suspect that perhaps at times she felt that way.

As she carried her vessel to the well, she also carried the weight of her burdens—of unresolved relationships and the hardships caused by them.

She must have been rejected by a few of these men. If they died, it could have felt like abandonment. We just don't know the details . Regardless, based on what we know of her she does not deserve our condemnation, but our compassion.

Jesus sees all of this. He sees her. And instead of stepping back, he leans in. He drinks water from her cup. He has a theologically rich and robust conversation with her. And then he reveals himself to her.

Christ crosses all geographical and cultural boundaries. He defies all expectations, laws, and obstacles to get to us.

To get to you. To get to me.

He is not put off by our past but is drawn to our present for the sake of our future.

He makes a point to right what has been wronged. He honors what has been shamed and what has been forgotten. There are no limits to his love.

It doesn't matter our circumstance, our gender, our financial status, our appearance, or our limits and lacks—these are not what he focuses on. They do not determine his proximity to us or his willingness to pursue us. Romans 8:39 reinforces this truth: "Neither height nor depth, nor anything else in all creation, will be able to separate us from the love of God that is in Christ Jesus our Lord."

Jesus makes radical choices to demonstrate a radical love.

Nothing stands in his way—not our deepest pain, not our heaviest burden, not our greatest sorrow.

Whatever rejection, abandonment, loneliness, or uncertainty we feel, it's not too much for him. He speaks directly to it with the mercy we so desperately need. He does not shame us.

We might say, "But, Lord, I have been so disappointed."

He would reply, "My child, I am faithful and steadfast, and I am love."

We might say, "But, Lord, I am so tired. I don't think I can try again."

He would reply, "Come to me, all who are weary and burdened, and I will give you rest."

We might say, "But, Lord, I have been left for dead and abandoned."

He would reply, "I bring the dead back to life. I restore what has been broken."

We might say, "But, Lord, no one cares! I have nothing to my name."

He would reply, "I call you beloved and blessed. Here is *my* name."

Jesus tells the woman, "If you knew the gift of God and who it is that asks you for a drink, you would have asked him and he would have given you living water" (John 4:10).

He tells her that this living water will become in her a spring of water welling up to eternal life.

He is that water—that boundless source of strength that offers us restoration and quenches our thirst.

In Colorado, we're graced with a few public hot springs you can visit and soak in. These natural bodies of water come up and out of the earth onto the surface from aquifers filled with snowmelt and rain. The heat in the hot springs comes from a geothermal gradient, which is just heat from deep inside Earth's interior.

I visited one recently with my friend Amber. Since she's a florist, she needed some help delivering and setting up her floral arrangements at a wedding in Salida. After spending all day decorating the venue, we had some time to drive up to Mount Princeton Hot Springs nearby.

That night, we relaxed in the pools of mineral-rich water as the sun set behind the mountains. The stars twinkled above in the cloudless sky as the water lapped gently at my hands. I reached down to the riverbed and grabbed the pebbles and dirt on the bottom and then let them fall back into the water. I felt around until I found three smooth stones to take home. I wanted to memorialize this moment. I felt grateful to be here.

During a lonely year, Amber had been a kind companion. She was the very picture of generosity, of giving without expecting anything in return. She had invited me along on this trip, paying the way for what, to me, felt like a big gulp of grace.

In the kindness of a friend, and in the simplicity of the moment, I caught a glimpse of what it felt like to receive the outpouring of refreshment from living water. Every bit of me that had felt raw and cracked were soothed.

Jesus meets us. He goes out of his way to bring himself to you. He breaks every barrier standing in his way to get to you so he can quench that thirst that bubbles from deep within.

Through a moment. Through a friend. Through an uncomplicated gesture.

His compassion does not run dry.

Neither does his goodness.

He has a place for you. He sees possibility in you.

The most profound moment between the woman and Jesus is when Jesus reveals himself to her: "The woman said, 'I know that Messiah' (called Christ) 'is coming. When he comes, he will explain everything to us.' Then Jesus declared, 'I, the one speaking to you—I am he'" (John 4:25–26).

Jesus trusts the woman with his identity.

She was not a problem in the eyes of Jesus. She was a placeholder—a representative of and a testament of who Jesus came for. Every one of us.

When Jesus reveals himself, the woman undergoes a transformation, like a metamorphosis of the heart.

As Jesus's disciples return with lunch, the woman leaves. She forgets the vessel she brought to carry her water. She leaves her burden behind. But she doesn't return home. She goes back into town.

Some translations say, "She ran."

I'm captivated by her response to the revelation of Jesus.

Nothing else mattered.

Whether she walked or leaped with joy, it's clear she had one motive: to tell as many people as she could about what Jesus had told her. "Can this be the Christ?" she asks them. Who else could love her as she was? "Come, see a man who told me everything I ever did" (John 4:29).

She forgot herself for the sake of others, all because of her encounter with Jesus.

In *The Freedom of Self-Forgetfulness*, Timothy Keller writes, "You see the verdict is in. And now I perform on the basis of the verdict. Because he loves me and he accepts me."[2]

Generosity comes from knowing you're not lacking.

Beth Moore, a revered Bible teacher, makes the point that this woman had no need for the vessel she left behind because she *herself* had become it.[3] She held the Living Water inside her, and it was overflowing from her—she could think of nothing else to do than share it.

We become what we thirst for. With Christ, we never run dry.

We give what we receive.

When we're full, we don't have to withhold.

To whom do we run back and tell of Christ?

To whom do we reflect Jesus's love?

On my thirtieth birthday, I decided to write my biological father a letter. After fifteen years of wrestling through the impact he had left on my life, I was ready to extend the same compassion and mercy that Christ had extended to me. After some serious sleuthing, I found what I believed to be his last known address.

I put pen to paper and wrote him about my life, about his grandchildren, and about how the Lord had dramatically changed me. At the end, I wrote—in so many words—"For what it's worth, I want you to know that I forgive you for the pain you have caused me and I pray that you can live the rest of your days in peace."

On the envelope, I did not put a return address. I wasn't ready to welcome him back into my life and knew, most likely, I never would be. But still I could feel the significance of this moment. I didn't know if the letter would ever make it to him, but I knew that I had been delivered—out of bitterness, sorrow, and pain.

This was my gift to my biological father, but it was also God's gift to me.

How do you bless the ones who have harmed you?

We cannot avoid forgiveness, though these days we seem to cringe at the suggestion of it. It is our first, although often delayed, response. We forgive not for the sake of another but for the sake of ourselves.

We're told in Colossians 3:13, "Bear with each other and forgive one another if any of you has a grievance against someone. Forgive as the Lord forgave you." The Greek word for forgiveness means "to let go." It means "to lose our record of wrongdoing that we might have for another."

Forgiveness is powerful. In fact, an act of forgiveness can restructure our brain. The neural networks that control our stress and pain receive a tangible dose of relief. Forgiveness acts as an antidote. It decreases depression, anxiety, anger, and even symptoms of PTSD.[4]

Forgiveness brings us back home to ourselves. It regulates our body, bringing it back to equilibrium.

I don't know if you've ever attempted to stand on one leg to balance, but sometimes it takes a minute—at least for me. We might lean to one side, trembling at first, and then finally find our center, arms outstretched, eyes set and focused. Forgiveness steadies us.

It's worth it, even if it isn't easy.

It doesn't always feel the way we want it to.

Sometimes it's just a decision. It's a belief that the benefits of letting go outweigh what might happen if we hold on. When forgiveness is withheld, so is closure. So we make the choice anyway. Forgiveness releases us and the ones we are forgiving from the past. It grants us both an untarnished future.

As a therapist, I have the opportunity to learn from a variety of wise people in the field. Once, one of them shared with me that trauma is a lot like having your body wedged within the frame of a door. You can't move because you have one foot set in the past even as the other ventures to walk through the other side. Rejection is like that. It can keep us stuck. And yet forgiveness softens us. It allows us to be more pliable, more flexible, and to stride more fully into the here and now.

It's the same for when we forgive ourselves.

When I ended my relationship with my best friend, I did feel some regret. In hindsight, I saw that I had made many of my choices through a lens of pain. I was angry with myself for pushing her away and not attempting to work through it.

I felt as if I had been drowning and found the closest thing to hold on to and inadvertently drowned it too.

Forgiveness isn't about looking at what was done and making excuses for it. We can't change what happened when we forgive. Rather, forgiveness changes us. It changes the way we feel about what happened and behave *because* of what happened.

I didn't just need to forgive myself for ending my friendship. I needed to forgive myself for every time I held back from pursuing my dreams or being my true self out of fear of failure and fear of being rejected by others. I had become so adept at getting in my own way, of letting self-sabotage govern me. I wanted to forgive myself for every belief I'd ever held that wasn't true.

Forgiveness gives us and others permission to rebuild from the rubble.

I imagine the Samaritan woman felt the same way about her life. I wonder if she thought she was a problem that needed to be solved. Whether or not we're responsible for what happens to us, we'll always find a way to blame someone or something. It's either us or them.

But Jesus saw her just as he sees us—plainly. He knows, and yet he forgives.

He gives us permission to renovate our lives and to start anew.

When the woman came back into her village, she gathered as many as she could around her and told them about Jesus. But she didn't not cry out that Jesus saw everything "they" had done to her. Instead, she said, "[He] told me everything I ever did" (John 4:29).

Eventually, we get to make a choice. Either we continue to live under the oppression of the memories of those who hurt us, or we choose to take responsibility for our hearts and souls.

Forgiveness can seem like cliché, which is why I now view it as an act of generosity. Each act require us to acknowledge what has already been given to us freely so that we can freely give to others.

We are blessed to bless. We get to be generous, to empty ourselves, and to give our lives to others.

I imagine you might be wondering about boundaries right about now.

Many of my relationships that have ended poorly haven't been repaired. I don't speak to them, and they don't speak to me. As with my biological dad, doing so didn't feel safe. I simply didn't trust them enough to invite them around.

We can honor our heart, and if it's still tender and bruised, we can make choices to protect it.

Boundaries are essential.

Thankfully, we talk about boundaries more now than we ever did. It used to be that, for some of us, we would let others step on us or push us around, or even subject ourselves to cruelty—all in the name of "being nice." Now, more and more, we tend to care about protecting our peace.

Yet I've also noticed that, as with other things, we've swung somewhat excessively to the other side of the extreme. We easily cut others out of our lives without ever coming back to revisit whether we're ready to give them another opportunity or without considering whether it's necessary.

Nowadays, because of politics and other points of passionate disagreement, we unfriend and unfollow those who bring out the worst in us. We don't usually stop to examine how we might position our hearts to love someone despite ongoing contention and tension.

We use boundaries as barricades—to keep people out.

What would it look like for generosity to coexist with boundaries?

Instead of walls, we could build bridges. We could safely welcome some of our most divisive relationships back into our lives. Not because they've changed, but because we have.

How often do we stop to scrutinize the boundaries we've created and then consider our motivations for creating them? Not always, but sometimes, we use what we can to justify a life that isn't actually hidden in Christ but instead is hidden in fear, bitterness, and frustration.

We shutter our windows and close our doors so we don't have to deal. We don't want to contend with anything hard or with ourselves. So we block, ignore, and mute whoever we want, whenever we want.

We're far more comfortable never speaking to or engaging with those who have hurt us. We're inclined to distance ourselves from anyone who isn't as healthy as we are, or who can't give as much, or who won't ever meet our expectations. We refuse to give room to those who challenge or vex us.

In the realm of generosity, we attach conditions to our giving. We become so concerned with our welfare that we retract ourselves from any relationships that require risk or feel too messy.

When we set boundaries that are too rigid or weaponized, we don't leave much room for Christ to work.

When I look at the life of Jesus and the way he set boundaries, what I see is a man who rested with God and then returned to the masses. He tended to his needs and humanity, but he always came back to lean in. We can do the same.

With boundaries, our measurement of health isn't about our capacity, but God's. This works on either end of the spectrum: boundaries that are too strict and those that are too loose. We don't have to protect our peace as if it's only ours to care for. We've got it all wrong. Rather, it's God's peace that protects us—we don't have anything to do with that except to learn from God.

When we step in tandem with God, we can be certain no one can step all over us. We're promised, "If God is for us, who can be against us?" (Rom. 8:31), and then we're asked, "Who is going to harm you if you are eager to do good? But even if you should suffer for what is right, you are blessed. 'Do not fear their threats; do not be frightened.' But in your hearts revere Christ as Lord" (1 Peter 3:13–15).

We are prompted to remember that being healed and whole—being safe, seen, and secure—we can engage with others distinctively. It pushes us to live a radical, unrecognizable, and maybe even offensive life.

Forgiveness doesn't mean we have to trust the people who have hurt us. Forgiveness is not excusing someone from accountability or consequence. It is not pretending we weren't hurt to begin with. Rather, forgiveness is putting Christ in his rightful place in our lives.

Generosity requires us to come out of hiding with open arms. It requires letting go, not holding on. That, in and of itself, is the etymology of the Greek word for forgiveness— *aphiemi*—which means "to send away."

All of this is made possible only by knowing who we are in Christ, abiding in him, and seeing Jesus as our living water. When we stand in a place of belovedness, we are standing in security. It doesn't matter how others might treat us or come at us—we can bless them the way Christ blesses us.

When Christ fills our cup, he is giving to us abundantly. That means we don't even have to attempt to fill ourselves on the crumbs of what others can give. We can extend ourselves toward them without starving and we can see others for who they are without being consumed with needing to be seen by them.

Christ's love serves as our boundary. It hems us in. It forms and shapes every part of who we were and are and the pieces of us that are still becoming. Christ unfurls the parts of us that would rather withhold, disappear, or run. He softens the sharper edges that have formed over years of being ignored and taken advantage of. He pursues us endlessly.

Christ liberates us from the prisons of unforgiveness, bitterness, and isolation, moving us toward those we'd rather avoid, ignore, or punish with silence. He helps us send away our desperation so we can be sent to testify to his mercy and goodness. Just as the woman dropped her water vessel, so we too can drop ours. We can lean freely into the relationships that are in front of us. We can give into them too.

I know it can be difficult to imagine what that might look like. But know that you can do all these things without compromising your safety, especially when you move at the Spirit's bidding. The Spirit will lead you to be wise about those with whom you can and should be generous and will embolden you to be unafraid.

When faced with someone who has turned against you, ask yourself this: How can I love them anyway?

You might write a letter to someone you haven't spoken with in a long time.

You might dedicate time to pray for them and bless them.

You might practice speaking well of them, especially in front of others.

You might serve them.

You might just leave the door open—giving room for other opportunities.

You might do the work to understand them and to exercise empathy and compassion.

You might find the will to let go of your expectations.

In these ways and more, we honor the God of reconciliation. We honor Christ as cup bearer and as living water. We allow ourselves to be a well instead of a broken vessel.

Oswald Chambers writes in *My Utmost for His Highest*, "Jesus did not say, 'He who believes in me will realize all the blessings of the fullness of God,' but in essence, 'He who believes in me will have everything he receives escape out of him.'" Chambers argues, "If we believe in Jesus, it is not what we gain but what he pours through us that really counts."[5]

Like Jesus, we can be vessels of humility that know God's glory and power. He doesn't leave us alone. That's what makes the impossible possible. It's how we can serve those who despise us and love those who have deceived us. We run in Christ's strength, not our own.

Jesus lived a life and suffered a death marked by rejection. Yet we remember him for his compassion and generosity. He is proof that we can be remembered that way too.

The more lost we are in the love of Jesus, the more we can become blind to the disappointment of others and the more we can love the unlovable. Time and time again, we will have to bring ourselves to Christ to fill up on the withness of Christ so we can go out and lose ourselves all over again. Matthew 4:4 (MSG) reminds us, "It takes more than bread to stay alive. It takes a steady stream of words from God's mouth."

And, in turn, we become people who see others because we are seen. Our generosity costs us nothing because it cost Christ everything. Love is a gift that we get to keep giving.

Retribution is in God's hands. We don't have to enact our own limited justice because we know that God will hold each of us accountable for our actions. We can speak truth. We can state what was done wrong. We can be honest about our hurt and pain. But justice isn't ours. It is God's.

As the psalmist writes, "For you, Lord, have delivered me from death, my eyes from tears, my feet from stumbling, that I may walk before the Lord in the land of the living" (Ps. 116:8–9).

The Lord gives us the freedom to lose ourselves. The outcome is not ours to secure.

~

Repair isn't a guarantee.

And generosity doesn't equate to restoration.

It's a conduit that allows us, at the very least, to aim for restoration—to direct our words and actions in a way that makes us more willing to give and receive, to let the Spirit do the work only he can manage to do.

None of this is meant to be laborious, back-breaking work. It's not meant to harm us either. But as much as it is up to us, we can check ourselves to see if we are moving toward others or away from them. We keep doing what we can, knowing that we can't change others or force their hands, yet still believing that generosity compounds.

Our experiences won't get the final say if we don't let them.

We only make them permanent if we're unwilling to relinquish them.

For me, I eventually had to let go of my biological dad. I had to stop tormenting myself over who he was to me, and who I thought I was because of him. I would never know why he left the way he did. I can't know how he felt. When someone is so taken by their addiction, they are only concerned for themselves.

Losing ourselves to Jesus allows us to accept those things that cannot be changed. Acceptance is the means by which we can grow in compassion and, eventually, in generosity.

I have come to accept that though I may never be able to change others, Christ can change me. And that—that is enough.

I could not change my dad, but I could aim to love him in the best way I knew how. I couldn't know what pain or suffering had made him turn to addiction and isolation. Some things aren't ours to know; they aren't ours to hold.

It feels uncomfortable to ask you to do what I myself still struggle to do. Aim for what? I wonder. What does it look like to lose myself here, with them?

Many of the broken relationships I've had over the years have remained unrepaired and unrestored. Some of them I hesitate to think could ever be different. Nor, I admit, do I want them to be. Why would I even try?

It's a matter of working out our faith. Forgiveness is the closest we can come to demonstrating the love of Christ. I believe it's what makes it feel so challenging.

All we can do is aim again and again to give as much as we can muster when we are given the opportunity to do so. Like Paul writes, "Not that I have already obtained all this, or have already arrived at my goal, but I press on to take hold of that for which Christ Jesus took hold of me" (Phil. 3:12).

We press on toward the upward call of Christ; not for perfection, but for progress.

Forgiveness and generosity aren't just a template to follow for when we've been hurt; they expand our capacity to love.

INHALE

On the cross you rescued me.

EXHALE

You were forsaken so I could belong.

BASED ON PSALM 22

CHAPTER 9

LAMA SABACHTHANI

I t was night, and the fire was blazing hot in our wood stove. The kids had fallen asleep, and all was quiet. I didn't think I could have this kind of life. I didn't think I could ever love or be loved quite this much. Rejection had lost. Christ had won.

Suddenly, the silence was interrupted by an obtrusive notification. I had just received a message from a distant cousin via social media. In it, she wrote that she was so sorry for my loss. Though I suspected I already knew, I asked her what had happened. What did she mean? Truth is, I had been waiting for this moment, had prayed that, though we had been separated, God would at least give me the opportunity to be told.

My dad had died.

So much time had been lost, time that I would never get back. I lamented what could have been and would never be. I grieved that this man who shared my nose and eyes no longer lived. Yet with his passing, I felt peace. I saw that I no longer looked within him for myself. I saw that my life that I once thought lacked so much was now rich in love.

I dialed my mom's number, and as in so many other conversations we had had before, I wondered aloud at how I was able to create a life that wasn't grounded in my dad's absence. I could have tried—and did try—to fill that void. But not once did it consume me. It did not overtake me.

Death is bittersweet. When I look back upon the people, places, and circumstances that could not or would not do life with me—though I wished differently—I honor the loss. It was, in sum, a gain.

When my dad abandoned me, it brought me to my knees. It made me ask questions of myself, of God, and of others.

When members of our church family turned their backs on us, I didn't think I'd survive. But what I knew of God became more robust, solid, and unrelenting.

When my friendships didn't last, it became clear that the only one who would never let me go was Christ. I learned to lean more on Jesus.

Every death involves an unshackling. It sets us free.

For every moment we've been spurned and for every time we've felt like we've died a little on the inside, we remember that what has been buried won't stay buried for long.

In the words of Greek poet Dinos Christianopoulos,

> what didn't you do to bury me,
> but you forgot that I was a seed.[1]

Jesus won't let you stay buried. Life always bursts through.

On the day Jesus hung on the cross, he had already bore the trauma of multiple physical beatings. In his humanity, he had prayed in anguish at the garden of Gethsemane, his sweat like drops of blood as he anticipated what was to come.

After Jesus was delivered into the hands of Pilate, he was presented to the whole battalion. They were there to witness his humiliation. They spat on him and whipped him, not with a simple rope, but with a wooden handle attached to three leather straps with pieces of metal, wire, glass, and fragments of bone tied to the ends.

They fastened a crown of thorns to sit atop his head, puncturing his skin to make it stay in place. Jesus—bruised, bloody, and barely able to move—was unrecognizable. "His appearance was so disfigured beyond that of any human being and his form marred beyond human likeness" (Isa. 52:14). Every lashing was a pronouncement of betrayal. Every stripe was a road to death that Jesus obediently walked. "He was wounded for our transgressions, he was bruised for our iniquities: the chastisement of our peace was upon him; and with his stripes we are healed" (Isa. 53:5 KJV).

And so drawing labored breaths, Christ hung from a cross.

Up to this point, he had yet to offer a complaint. He received it all: Judas's betrayal, Peter's denial, the crowd's judgment, Pilate's decision, and the disciples' scattering; the disciples hid from the people they were certain would kill them too.

At midday, the sky darkened. The sun disappeared. With a cry, an outpouring of anguish, Jesus asked, "My God, my God, why have you forsaken me?" (Matt. 27:46).

His words disquiet our souls. They bear witness to the ones who have felt rejected and betrayed. When we feel unseen or have been abandoned, we know intimately Christ's overture.

God doesn't ever leave us, but at times it can feel as if he has.

Our pain may never compare to what Christ endured, but our questions are similar. They echo what we have silently asked and wondered, afraid to voice our fears.

Where are you, God?

Why did you leave me?

Why did they desert me?

I am alone.

I imagine Christ pushing himself up with his feet and the backs of his arms—unable to move his pierced wrists—to make this plea. For him to do so could only indicate that, at this moment, he felt the weight of rejection, of forsakenness.

Where he once was swaddled and cherished by his mother and father, then doted on by kings and shepherds as the hope of the world, the Messiah now hung naked and alone. He did not call for his Father. He called for his God. There's an absence here. Not once until this moment did Jesus refer to God as his God.

Jesus calls us back to the verse of Psalm 22, echoing the very words that David once spoke.

The best way I can understand this is that at this moment,

Christ felt utter desolation from the loss of the intimacy he had with his Father. He felt the break of God's presence.

Though still loved, Christ felt as if God had withdrawn from him as he carried the sin and suffering of the world. Christ went without the presence of his Father so we could experience a life with him, so God's presence might never leave us.

No one came to Christ's rescue, no one saved him, and no one spoke up for him.

But Jesus wasn't looking to be saved. It was in this moment that Jesus would become our Savior. This rejection, this forsakenness, was key to what would come for him and for us. He willingly suffered.

Surrendered to the devastation of his body and to the burden of carrying our sorrow and sin, like the light of a candle flickering as it fades, the Light of the World was snuffed out. Death consumed him.

Arms stretched wide, Christ hangs at the place where we can move across and over what has felt for so long like an obstacle to our healing. Rejection served as a bridge to resurrection—so that what feels like death to us, and what was certainly death to Christ, offers us an invitation to new life.

The words of 2 Corinthians 5:16–17 put it aptly: "From now on we regard no one from a worldly point of view. Though we once regarded Christ in this way, we do so no longer. Therefore, if anyone is in Christ, the new creation has come. The old has gone, the new is here!"

For our sake, Christ was forsaken so we could live a life of reconciliation. Though sin separated us, Christ reunited us. He repaired our broken relationship with God. He gives us a template in which we can repair our relationships with others.

When we are reconciled to God, our lives change. By his forgiveness and his presence, we are never alone. More importantly, Christ makes us whole.

As we live in this space some call the "now and the not yet," we can be certain that we will continue to experience the disappointment of others. We will be treated as less than. We will experience the deep wounds that only the people closest to us can inflict. We might be publicly humiliated or canceled. We might be made to face a battalion of people who mock us and want the worst for us. We might be judged harshly for the very things we hold close—whether our culture, our faith, our race, our gender, or our character.

Our most intimate relationships may feel unsteady, wracked with a history of mistrust, betrayal, or estrangement. Rejection, we know, is unavoidable, built into this present life. But Jesus's words and actions on the cross give us hope that, though rejection is inevitable, it is not insurmountable.

For the exiled, marginalized, excluded, and overlooked, the darkness that veiled the world as Jesus cried out to God is an invitation to know Christ, to know that he knows us—that the betrayal and rejection we have experienced are things he shares with us.

Christ's death wasn't remarkable. It was common. Thousands of people had been crucified before him.

Crucifixion was gruesome, and terrible, but it was used regularly by the Romans to punish and intimidate. Rejection itself isn't remarkable either. We know its frequency, but we take comfort in knowing that Jesus knows our agony intimately. He doesn't ask us to carry what he hasn't already carried. But he invites us in to see who we get to be because of his sacrifice. Our lives are held by arms pierced with nails. His scars, the same ones that Thomas touched after Jesus rose from the dead, bear the truth that even our worst suffering cannot hold us back.

Because of him we can live a new life, one that doesn't stay weighed down beneath the power of the words or actions of those who have hurt us or left us. We are risen with Christ—transformed.

It's Jesus's resurrection that completes this story—our story.

Jesus's rejection begins what will accomplish the unthinkable: Jesus resurrection from the dead. That is what redeems, restores, and reconciles us to God.

What Christ did for us wasn't only to secure our future. It was also meant to hold our past and present. He came that we could live our lives abundantly, lacking nothing and at peace with God.

When Nash was younger, he developed a fear of water. For years, bath time was torture—for all of us. When it came time to wash his face and hair, he'd fight us, resisting the necessity of being submerged or even having the water poured over top of him. We could not convince him that he would not drown. We could only be patient—he needed time to work it out on his own.

One day, Nash turned to me and said, "I want to be baptized." It took me by surprise. I hadn't known that he had been processing this decision—but he was confident. He wanted to make Jesus the Lord of his life. I was overjoyed. But I knew that in order to be baptized he would have to overcome his fear of water. He would have to immerse himself in that which scared him the most to commit himself to what he loved more.

Sunday came. Outside, Nash sat in the trough of water with his dad at his side. As Ethan talked him through the process—reminding him to plug his nose and close his eyes—I could tell he was eager to begin. He was nervous, asking his dad, "Will you warn me first?" We all laughed, and Ethan reassured him that he would.

We're never prepared for the hardships that come our way. We don't often welcome them. The dark is only ever dark to us. But when we know that we get Jesus, we feel braver—maybe a little more willing to work through our dread.

We know that at some point we will come up and out the other side—up from that tepid water with a deep breath, filling our lungs with oxygen and joy.

Ethan dunked Nash, holding his head, reassuring him that even submerged, he would not be allowed to drown. Then he pulled him up and into his arms. Nash beamed. He had moved through his fear to find love.

We can move from death to life after rejection. We might

start by holding our breath for fear of the worst, but when we come to life in Christ, we can exhale.

∽

Jesus spoke only a few words on the day he died. Yet his last words were not of his forsakenness, but of his surrender. Calling out with a loud voice one last time, he said, "Father, into your hands I commit my spirit" (Luke 23:46). He breathed his last breath—of obedience and acceptance. He yielded up his spirit.

In the same way, Jesus invites us to let go of our old self and past hurts.

Why would we choose to live dead when we can live fully alive?

As Christ is forsaken, we're received. And as he is emptied out, we are filled. For many of us, this truth endears us to hope. For others, like me, it ends our striving. When we live from abundance it means we're able to take the risk of being rejected, to take the risk of being seen and of being loved as we truly are.

We want to avoid rejection, but in many ways, it is the only path to life.

In a podcast I regularly listen to produced by the Allender Center, I remember the host saying once that "every life reveals something of the death of Jesus." Our lives reveal that rejection isn't the end. This death is temporary. We can take our broken hearts and wrap them in linen cloth, scent them with myrrh, set them within a tomb, and know they will be raised again.

Tombs like the one Christ was buried in were used as a permanent resting place for the dead. The stone that shrouded the entryway was immovable for one person alone. And the bodies of the dead were customarily wrapped elaborately. The hands and feet were tied together with strips of cloth. Freedom couldn't have been made more impossible from death and from the grave.

In the same way Christ was set in the tomb, our broken hearts are too—our hands and feet tied, rendered immovable.

Yet Christ rose. He came back to life. When his friends came looking for him, the stone had been rolled away, and his body was missing.

The angel asked them, "Why do you look for the living among the dead" (Luke 24:5). Why do we look for safety and security in what has been broken and destroyed? We won't find them there. Why do we look for fullness in the affirmation of others when we know it cannot be sustained?

When Jesus gave up his life, when he moved through rejection for us, he broke the power that rejection has over our lives. His death became the invitation to the kingdom, and to freedom.

Our invitation extends to the table.

Isaiah 25:6–8 describes it best: "On this mountain the LORD Almighty will prepare a feast of rich food for all peoples, a banquet of aged wine—the best of meats and the finest of wines. On this mountain he will destroy the shroud that enfolds all peoples, the sheet that covers all nations; he will swallow up death forever. The Sovereign LORD will wipe away the tears from all faces; he will remove his people's disgrace from all the earth."

We all want a seat at the table. Tables imply plenty, abundance, and favor. It's where we sit to find connection, presence, and provision. Sometimes the table is where decisions are made and where we see that we belong.

Yet rejection has a way of making us think that there isn't any room for us at all.

We think we have to fight for our place; that we have to negotiate our status.

But we don't. When Christ died on the cross, he didn't just make room for us. He chose to save a spot for us. He etched our name on it and made it ours. His invitation to us wasn't by obligation, but with determination and desire. There isn't anyone who can steal what rightfully belongs to us—what was given to us.

Even in the presence of our enemies, we can sit and rest at the table (Ps. 23:5).

What is for you is already yours.

INHALE

I once was dead,

EXHALE

But in Christ, I now live.

BASED ON ROMANS 6:8–12

CHAPTER 10

WHERE, O DEATH, IS YOUR VICTORY?

In "The Mad Farmer Manifesto," Wendell Berry, novelist and poet, writes fervently for a revolution of sorts. He casts vision for a life that might be lived fully alive, instead of hopeless and dead. It's counterintuitive, and a call to revive the mind and spirit.[1]

I can't remember when I first stumbled upon Berry's words, but they came at a time where I thought perhaps, I might not ever find a resolution to the problem of rejection, if there was one.

As I read each stanza over and over again, a final and definitive shift happened within me. Berry's words grasped the defiance of a life lived in Christ, and the freedom we receive when we surrender to our heart's yearning for connection. More so, I realized that I didn't have to solve anything.

Such lines as "So, friends, every day do something that won't compute" and "Be joyful though you have considered all the facts" challenge and convict.

But for me, no line stood out more than this one: "Love someone who doesn't deserve it." And then with a flourish Berry ends with this imperative:

Practice Resurrection.

I couldn't shake it. What could our lives look like if *this* was our response to, well, *anything*? But especially rejection? What if we allowed to act as if we could always begin anew?

Wendell Berry is prompting us to remember that we are not only witnesses *to* but participants *in* Christ's resurrection. The same power that raised Jesus from the dead lives within us and is available to us (Eph. 1:19–20).

On this phrase, Eugene Peterson comments, "We live our lives in the practice of what we do not originate and cannot anticipate. When we practice resurrection, we continuously enter into what is more than we are. When we practice resurrection, we keep company with Jesus, alive and present, who knows where we are going better than we do, which is always 'from glory to glory.'"[2]

With Christ, possibility abounds. With Christ, we get to ask ourselves: How might we engage with rejection if we're anchored in his life and resurrection?

Could we love those who don't deserve it?

Could we exchange our disappointment and pain for an outpouring of grace?

Could we give ourselves to others without expectation?

Could we live lives that simply don't make sense?

To each of these, the answer is an unequivocal yes. And every yes is an act of courage, a step toward fully embodying a life in which we are held and beloved by Jesus.

Courage requires intention, and for some of us, it also requires change. Change can feel impossible at times. Yet change is a continuum, a sum of our choices made time and time again. This is why resurrection must become a practice, a daily intention of returning to what we know is true about ourselves because of Christ.

Jesus's impact on us is deeply spiritual, but it is also significantly practical and tangible. He serves as a guide, our way to wholeness. He serves as the context in which we see our lives.

When it comes to change, context matters. As does repetition and formation.

When our environment or our understanding of something shifts, this leads to a change in our behavior. Both our surroundings and our knowledge of them usually cue us to act appropriately.

For example, how we act in our homes is different from how we act at the gym or the library. We know the rules we're supposed to follow. Though they're often implied, we abide by them. Context gives us meaning. We know what to expect from each of these spaces as soon as we enter them.

Cues work, like key details, alongside context to give us more information. They help us to remember. When I set my running shoes out, I am prompting myself to go for a jog. Cues tell us to do, to change, to grow, and to act.

When Christ is the context and the resurrection our cue, both come together as an instruction to live from what Jesus is capable of. We don't operate as if we're living from our limited world, but from the limitlessness of the kingdom of God. It's made possible then for us to actually practice what we've seen Jesus do. To be brought out of death and into life.

We were made for new.

Our bodies reflect this truth.

Neuroplasticity mirrors resurrection, and renewal. Plasticity is the brain's ability to form new neurons, make fresh connections, and reshape or dismantle others. It is all the evidence we need to know that change is possible. Inside our brains, nerve cells are always transmitting data from one another. These neurons hold our histories and everything we have ever known. Within this network, we'll find all the stories we are told repeatedly—the ones we believe most ardently. Each neuron carves out it's understanding of our world.

What we practice habitually becomes what we know most intimately. Every time we respond to a person, a place, or circumstance we are either repeating what we already know or changing it. Neurons translate these habits. Though they've formed a path, they're used to using we can redirect them. We can help them create more helpful connections.

Neuroplasticity shows us how we've become who we are, but it also reveals that we're free to become who we want to be. We can become who we were made to be.

184

When we put ourselves in Christ's hands, we begin to think less like ourselves and more like him, obsessing less of what was and more of what can be.

Practicing resurrection, and living by it, is the spiritual plasticity in which Christ rewires our neurons, resuscitates our hearts, and lets our stories be rewritten. It is the very act by which you are "transformed by the renewing of your mind. Then you will be able to test and approve what God's will is—his good, pleasing and perfect will" (Rom. 12:2).

We get to engage in this process. "[We] put on the new self, created to be like God in true righteousness and holiness" (Eph. 4:24).

Practicing resurrection is a practice of spiritual formation. We get to make a choice to change our daily rhythms and responses to reflect what we know to be true about who we get to be. We get to live our lives, even as we navigate rejection, from an overflow of hope.

First, we practice death. In order for something to be brought back to life, we have to be willing to let it go, to let it die.

During that summer of wildflowers, I regrettably neglected my own flower boxes in the backyard. They filled with weeds and grass, the overgrowth escaping each side. There just wasn't any time to tend to them. Then, out of one box, three thick stalks began to grow. I didn't water them. I hardly paid any attention to them until I saw the petals unfurl, reaching toward the sun. These sunflowers had come out of nowhere and flourished without attention. At least that's how it seemed. Then, one day, my mother-in-law suggested that most likely the birds had planted the seeds.

As they ate from the bird feeder that stood beside the flower boxes, they must have dropped the excess seeds into the soil. I was stunned. It struck me—God had planted those seeds. He had grown those flowers. He had brought back to life what I was certain was dead.

God does the same in our lives. We don't have to keep our hands full, or constantly working. We can trust that God is interceding, even as we relinquish what we thought only we could keep alive. God is in every beginning, and every ending. In knowing this, in knowing what we mean to him, we can surrender. We *can* let go.

What is gaining our life if we have yet to lose it?

How do we begin to receive if our hands are still full?

Countless times, I have had to surrender my idea of what I wanted my life to look like and who I wanted to shared it with. I have sat with so many others who have experienced the same. I think of those who suffer from a chronic illness who have yet to find relief. Or of those who are navigating infertility. I think of those who are eager for a spouse—to be married—but their singleness persists. Or those whose marriages seem to be on the brink of divorce—documents ready to be signed, sealed, and delivered.

We will have friendships that end and never begin again. Parents who die. Interactions with individuals who refuse to repair what they have broken. Opportunities that won't come back around. Choices that we only got one chance to make.

It's harsh, but true.

Even as life delivers these blows, may you know that letting go isn't the same as losing hope.

Letting go is relinquishing our grip on the way we think things should be. For the moment, at least.

Letting go is taking hold of Christ's invitation to be transformed. We let him tend to the soil of our hearts; those places that are overgrown with weeds, like my flower boxes. Here, God reshapes, restructures, and repairs. We learn that our stories aren't over, *even if* our dreams seem to be.

Resurrection is God's business. Not ours.

We only have so much control, and most of it lies in our response.

We start with prayer. It is a posture of dependence and of letting go.

It is also where we learn to receive.

When we're praying, the areas of our brain that are involved in taking action are deactivated. This means that during prayer, we're not focused on controlling our environment. We're able to self-reflect and self-soothe. Our reactivity is lowered. We're more inclined to think beyond ourselves. Prayer activates our frontal lobe, which is connected to focus and attention. This region also helps regulate our emotions and reduce our stress.

Neuroscientist Andrew Newberg says that because there is less activity in the parietal lobe, the region that controls our sense of space and time, people who pray experience a greater sense of oneness, even transcendence.

We're literally tuning everything out to gaze on one thing: God.[3]

Prayer is also responsible for stimulating serotonin and dopamine. These messengers tell the body how to work and feel. Serotonin makes us feel good, makes us calm. Dopamine helps us to feel satisfied and motivated. Prayer is an accessible way to increase both in our lives.

It is without a doubt that prayer changes us.

Not only does it move our bodies out of fight-or-flight mode so we can become more intentional, but it also serves as a conduit for rewiring our brains.

Instead of focusing on what we used to know, prayer expands our attention. It directs us toward truth and toward a loving God.

Prayer invites us to connect and to lead lives of connection.

Newberg found that prayer strengthens a specific neural circuit that allows us to more freely access empathy and compassion. When we are changed, we can take part in being the change for others too. Prayer is what leads us to aim our lives toward others.

Just twelve minutes of prayer each day can make a profound impact on our brains. Twelve minutes—that's all it takes.[4]

It takes very little to be changed by Christ.

Or to embody a life of resurrection.

We don't pray simply to be changed. We pray knowing we're being listened to. Christ himself sits at the right hand of God, interceding for us (Rom. 8:34).

When we pray, we're acknowledging Jesus's power, authority, and glory. When we pray, we recognize we have an advocate in him.

He is thinking of us. He is thinking of you.

One of my dear friends, Bethny, reminds me of this.

Every time it was clear that God was working out something for my good, I could hear her joy over the phone as she asked, "How does it feel to be God's favorite?"

For a while, I would brush her comment off. It made me feel uncomfortable.

I certainly didn't feel like his favorite when I could see the lack, the trouble, and the pain. But like John, the "disciple Jesus loved," I came to see Bethny's question for what it was—a declaration of the love that displayed itself on the cross for me. Through prayer, I can see clearly who I am to God.

I can see that he is for me, undoubtedly.

He cherishes us. His life and death and resurrection tell us so.

How does it feel to be the apple of God's eye? Might you let that change you.

When we pray, we're not mumbling meaningless words to a distant God.

Prayer is connection. It connects our hearts to our minds, our minds to our bodies, and our bodies to our responses. It connects us to God.

It keeps us tender, soft, and pliable. Though we often have our palms closed together in prayer, our hearts burst wide open with surrender.

In its purest form, prayer is an opportunity to be loved as we are.

Love frees us. It compels us to live radically. It makes us strive to live in accordance with Wendell Berry's advice to "love someone who doesn't deserve it."

It goes right up against what comes naturally to us. But in practicing resurrection, we are embracing our new self, not our old one.

We're not supposed to act natural, but supernatural.

Jesus commands us, "But to you who are listening I say: Love your enemies, do good to those who hate you, bless those who curse you, pray for those who mistreat you" (Luke 6:27–28).

Jesus's words give us a target at which to aim.

I have several friends who still attend the church we left. One of them happened to invite us to her wedding, which was held in the church's sanctuary. Though I knew I wanted to attend, I wasn't sure how I could return to the building that held so many memories. Everyone would be there, including the old staff.

As we entered the foyer, familiarity coursed through my body. I was immediately confronted with people whose silence and apathy had betrayed me.

And then *there they were*, the ones I had held most responsible.

I thought I would feel angrier. I thought I would feel the impulse to run.

It never came.

Even after they walked right by me. Even after another person felt they could be rude.

All I felt was peace. It wasn't love; it was a capacity to

see them as able to be loved and blessed and prayed for. They were no longer my enemies.

When we truly experience the power of the cross, we begin to grow a little bit softer. We see people through a lens of sacrifice, not one of self-protection.

Practicing resurrection allows us to mature in our faith. It allows us to live our lives with hope. It changes our perspective of the world. It's what makes it possible for me to remain open to reconciliation with those who have hurt me. It's what has allowed me to repair my relationship with an imperfect system. It's what keeps me showing up and pressing in.

We certainly won't always get it right. We may have to take the smallest steps to get there. But we're simply aiming for what we know is possible, not through us but through Christ.

When we need a start, we can turn to the template that Jesus handed us.

We can pray,

> Your kingdom come.
> Your will be done.

And we can personalize our plea:

> In this church.
> With these people.
> In my heart.

We turn our attention not to the past or the future, but to the here and now.

We see the Lord's agenda instead of staying stuck in our own.

We can pray that our hearts will be made ready for such a time as when we might stumble into someone at a coffee shop or find that they've been interjected into our lives in some way or another once again—that we would be so immersed in Christ that we can love them even if they don't know how to love us back.

We can also prepare our hearts. We can start by intentionally pouring into others without expectation. We can let new habits form our love for others and form us.

When Ethan and I were married, we bought a unity candle to light after we said our vows. To the wax, I pinned a few words C. S. Lewis wrote: "Love is a deep unity, maintained by the will and deliberately strengthened by habit; reinforced by the grace which both partners ask, and receive, from God." Lewis captures the essence of what love can be—something to build with intention.

There are many ways we can do this.

We can regularly reach out to people as they come to mind—to check in with them or encourage them. We can remember them. And to let them know we did. With our mouths, we can speak words that bring life to those we're speaking to.

We can be someone who tends to the needs of others, looking for what they might not even be able to see. Perhaps we bring a meal to a family whose life is full, or we volunteer at a local nonprofit that serves our community. We might drop off a cup of coffee for a coworker or our child's teacher—especially when we might feel some contention with them.

In conversation, we can take the role of someone who asks questions—who chooses to go much deeper than just the weather. We can remain focused on the other person, unconcerned with ourselves. Unless they ask. Then we engage fully and wholeheartedly.

We can purposely strike up conversations with those we might usually ignore—the cashier, the barista, or the older gentleman you pass every week on your morning walk.

We can take the time to really see someone and, in that limited time, try to know them. We are all Jesus's beloved. We so often forget to treat each other as such.

It's not about being perfect so much as it is about making progress.

It's about making an effort to move from love, not for it.

Who is it we need to move toward? Who comes to mind?

Another way we can practice resurrection is seeing both the possibility and the good that reside in another human, even when those things coexist with brokenness, hurt, or misunderstanding.

For example, at the height of my insecurities and when I felt like I most questioned the love of my husband, I began a list.

I began to jot down the goodness in him and the goodness I saw in our relationship. Where did he try? Where in our marriage did we thrive? I'd read it back to myself every so often as a reminder that we were not without hope. Now I can see myself and our marriage in a better light. I know where we're both making an effort, where we're both working in tandem to love each other well.

Abundance is a matter of perspective.

We have what we need to be able to give to others and to be present with them. We're more capable than we think to do what is difficult—to attend to even those people we might despise. We don't have to be blinded by our own needs any longer. They've been met and will continue to be.

Resurrection is a miracle. It is counter to everything we know.

Our response gets to be too.

We're able to believe in the impossible simply because we know the impossible is true. And we can "be steadfast, immovable, always abounding in the work of the Lord, knowing that in the Lord [our] labor is not in vain" (1 Cor. 15:58 ESV). He wastes nothing.

Resurrection gives us hope, and hope secures us. It ties us down and keeps us steady when everything around us attempts to run us off. Hope compels us to take risks and to move toward the dark as the light shines brightly within us.

We may face ongoing rejection, we may see relationships fall apart, we may be weary at how we get in our own way, but hope isn't found in our striving; it's found in our relationship with Christ. We keep showing up—to ourselves and to others, but always and especially to him.

We know that every little death we die will only make us more alive.

Rejection is our way through. We don't have to avoid or fear this pain, because we know how this story ends, if not for them, at least for us.

So then, we take the hand of Christ and grip tight, knowing that he keeps us safe. He sees us. He comforts us in our suffering. He delivers us.

We are his beloved—never forsaken and never alone.

ACKNOWLEDGMENTS

While rejection has shaped me, so has belonging—I have not lacked in friendship or love.

For even when I felt as if I was alone, I was not.

Bethny, when I called you that day to tell you that I thought I needed to start over—to write a different book, an honest one—you weren't afraid to tell me the truth. You never are. You are both a force to be reckoned with and a safe haven. I am forever grateful that we found each other. It is a privilege to call you my friend.

K.J., you see others so clearly, through a lens of abundance, not scarcity. It is, without a doubt, because of your encouragement that I am where I am as a writer and creative. Thank you for embodying courage, compassion, and tenacity. Thank you for leading the way with kindness and generosity. Thank you for believing in me even when I did not believe in myself.

To my kind and wonderful literary agent, Ingrid Beck,

you are a gift. If life and death are in the power of the tongue, you have spoken nothing but life over me. For every doubt and insecurity I had, you steadied me with your wisdom and optimism. When I wanted to give up, you kept me moving forward. Thank you. I couldn't have done any of this without you.

To the team at Zondervan Reflective, thank you for taking a risk on someone as unknown as me. You have been a dream come true.

Jennifer Ericksen, although we've seen the worst together, I know the best is yet to come. From the very beginning, you have reminded me of this over and over again, not just with your words but with your life. With every choice, you show your belief in a God who really is chasing after all of us with goodness and mercy. It has changed me, and I am forever grateful.

Countless people have come alongside me on this journey through the years, and stayed.

Cassandra Speer, you refreshed my weary soul every time we were together. Lindsay Falls and April Payne, you held up my arms when I could no longer bear the weight of failure. Lisa Hensley, Breanne Rodgers, Pricelis Perreaux-Dominguez, Kaitlin Chappell Rogers, and Phylicia Masonheimer—in a variety of ways, you have each come alongside me and given me the strength to keep going, to keep trying, and to keep my eyes on the Lord. Amber Mustain, your benevolence is a blessing to all who know you. Nicole Frederick, the invitation you extended to me years ago was the catalyst for a bold request and then answered prayer.

I'll never forget it. Patrick and Lanitha Tanton, you were a refuge for Ethan's and my tired souls when we didn't know where to go. Each of you, and so many others, have been God's kindness to me.

To my clients, the work we do together is hard and holy. It's an honor to be a part of your story.

Mom, I owe my resiliency to you. You exemplified dedication and service, and I learned what it meant to persevere by watching you. You showed me what it looked like to follow Jesus —from the margins, behind the scenes, and with faithful obedience. You laid the groundwork that I get to flourish in. Thank you.

To all my family, your support is everything.

Special thanks to Jenn Panariso who encouraged me in the moments I most needed it.

To Nash, Glory, and Levi, being your mom is the best thing I'll ever do. You make me better. Nash, I see the world with so much more delight and gratitude because of your curiosity and wonder. You make anything seem possible. Glory, you hold nothing back. Because of you, I'm learning not to, either. Levi, your tender heart reminds me to stay soft. You've never met a stranger, and you encourage me to love others like that too.

Ethan, you are the love of my life. It is to my utter dismay that though you know the worst of me, you continue to stand by my side. You are unwavering in your loyalty. For all the loss I have experienced, it compares little to the gain I have had in being your best friend and wife.

Finally, I am, if nothing else, formed through the grace

of Jesus. Without him, this book would not exist. For every moment I shrunk in fear, he declared the truth: I am his beloved. It was his love that emboldened me, guided me, and sustained me.

Jesus, you have never forsaken me. You never will.

NOTES

CHAPTER 1: INEVITABLE DEMISE

1. Kristin Weir, "The Pain of Social Rejection," *APA Monitor on Psychology* 43, no. 4 (April 2012): 50, https://www.apa.org/monitor/2012/04/rejection.

2. Bregtje Gunther Moor, Eveline A. Crone, and Maurits W. van der Molen, "The Heartbrake of Social Rejection: Heart Rate Deceleration in Response to Unexpected Peer Rejection," *Psychological Science* 21, no. 9 (2010), doi:10.1177/0956797610379236.

3. Daniel J. Siegel, *The Power of Showing Up: How Parental Presence Shapes Who Our Kids Become and How Their Brains Get Wired* (New York: Ballantine, 2020).

CHAPTER 2: EVIDENCE OF THINGS NOT SEEN

1. Gabor Maté, *The Myth of Normal: Trauma, Illness, and Health in an Insane Culture* (Toronto: Penguin Random House Canada, 2022), 31.

2. Richard C. Schwartz, *Internal Family Systems Therapy*, 2nd ed. (New York: Guilford, 2019).

CHAPTER 3: LOYAL IN HIS LOVE

1. Nicole Lipkin, "Our Brains Want to Be Lazy: Here's How to Win the Battle," *Forbes*, October 25, 2022, https://www.forbes.com/sites/nicolelipkin/2022/10/25/our-brains-want-to-be-lazy-heres-how-to-win-the-battle/.
2. Kelly M. Kapic, *A Little Book for New Theologians* (Downers Grove, IL: IVP Academic, 2012), 30.
3. A. W. Tozer, *The Knowledge of the Holy: The Attributes of God* (n.p.: Fig, 2017), 36.
4. Deb Dana, *Polyvagal Exercises for Safety and Connection: 50 Client-Centered Practices* (New York: Norton, 2020), 108–10.
5. Elizabeth Barrett Browning, *Aurora Leigh*, 7th ed. (London: Capman and Hall, 1865), book 7, 304.
6. Terrance Klein, "Rejection Is Part of Life—Even for God," *America Magazine*, January 26, 2022, https://www.americamagazine.org/faith/2022/01/26/jesus-nazareth-rejection-good-word-242288.
7. Alejandra Borunda, "2023: Year of the Superbloom," *National Geographic*, January 18, 2023, https://www.nationalgeographic.com/environment/article/2023-year-of-the-superbloom-flowers-california.

CHAPTER 4: IN THE WILDERNESS

1. Dietrich Bonhoeffer, *The Cost of Discipleship* (New York: Touchstone, 2012), 89.
2. F. B. Meyer, *Christ in Isaiah: Expositions of Isaiah 40–55* (New York: Revell, 1895), 34.

CHAPTER 5: GRAVEN IMAGES

1. Timothy Keller, *Counterfeit Gods: The Empty Promises of Money, Sex, and Power, and the Only Hope That Matters* (New York: Penguin, 2009), xix.

2. Diane Langberg, *Redeeming Power: Understanding Authority and Abuse in the Church* (Grand Rapids: Brazos, 2020), 31.

3. Timothy Keller, *Center Church: Doing Balanced, Gospel-Centered Ministry in Your City* (Grand Rapids: Zondervan, 2012), 127.

4. Charles Haddon Spurgeon, *Morning and Evening: Daily Readings*, ed. Alistair Begg (Wheaton, IL: Crossway, 2003), November 19, evening.

5. Hannah Hurnard, *Hinds' Feet on High Places: An Engaging Visual Journey*, illustrated by Jill de Haan (Carol Stream, IL: Tyndale, 2021), 34.

6. Jack Hayford, "A Time of Altars," Jack Hayford Ministries, https://www.jackhayford.org/teaching/articles/a-time-of-altars/.

7. My summary of Arielle Schwartz's ideas in *The Post-Traumatic Growth Guidebook: Practical Mind-Body Tools to Heal Trauma, Foster Resilience, and Awaken Your Potential* (Berkeley: North Atlantic, 2020).

8. Steffany Gretzinger, "Pieces," recording by Bethel Music, *Have It All*, 2016, track 7, Redding, CA.

CHAPTER 6: IN GOOD COMPANY

1. Sharon Hodde Miller (@SHoddeMiller), Instagram, August 17, 2023, summarizing Henri J. M. Nouwen, *The Wounded Healer: Ministry in Contemporary Society* (Garden City, NY: Doubleday, 1972).

2. Frederick Buechner, *Wishful Thinking: A Seeker's ABC* (New York: HarperOne, 1993), 15.

3. Kristen Neff and Christopher Germer, *The Mindful Self-Compassion Workbook: A Proven Way to Accept Yourself, Build Inner Strength, and Thrive* (New York: Guilford, 2018).

4. Barbora Kucerova, Nava Levit-Binnun, Ilanit Gordon, and Yulia Golland, "From Oxytocin to Compassion: The Saliency of Distress," *Biology* 12, no. 2 (2023): 183, https://doi.org/10.3390/biology12020183.

5. Timothy Keller, *The Freedom of Self-Forgetfulness* (New York: 10Publishing, 2012), 40.

CHAPTER 7: RITUALS OF HUMILITY

1. Charles Haddon Spurgeon, "Jesus Wept," *The Spurgeon Archive*, July 23, 1989, https://www.spurgeon.org/resource-library/sermons/jesus-wept/#flipbook/.

2. X. Lei, Y. Wu, M. Xu, et al. "Physical Exercise: Bulking up Neurogenesis in Human Adults," *Cell Bioscience* 9 (2019): 74, https://doi.org/10.1186/s13578-019-0337-4.

3. NPR Staff, "Anne Lamont Distills Prayer into 'Help, Thanks, Wow," *Morning Edition*, NPR, November 19, 2012, https://www.npr.org/2012/11/19/164814269/anne-lamott-distills-prayer-into-help-thanks-wow.

4. Cardinal Rafael Merry del Val, Litany of Humility, prayer, 1867.

CHAPTER 8: LOSE YOURSELF

1. Kristi McLelland, *Jesus and Women: Video Series*, session 3, companion to the book *Jesus and Women: In the First Century and Now* (Nashville: Lifeway, 2019).

2. Timothy Keller, *The Freedom of Self-Forgetfulness* (Chorley, UK: 10publishing, 2012), 40.

3. Beth Moore, "Meet Me at the Well," sermon, Living Proof Ministries, YouTube video, 1:05:30, August 11, 2020, https://www.youtube.com/watch?v=W9RrMK0fX8U.

4. "Forgiveness: Your Health Depends on It," *Johns Hopkins Medicine*, https://www.hopkinsmedicine.org/health /wellness-and-prevention/forgiveness-your-health-depends -on-it.

5. Oswald Chambers, *My Utmost for His Highest* (Uhrichsville, OH: Barbour, 2015), September 2.

CHAPTER 9: LAMA SABACHTHANI

1. Dinos Christianopoulos, *The Body and the Wormwood (1960–1993)*, ed. A. Boutopoulou, trans. N. Kostis (n.p., 1995).

CHAPTER 10: WHERE, O DEATH, IS YOUR VICTORY?

1. Wendell Berry, "The Mad Farmer Manifesto," in *The Mad Farmer Poems* (Berkeley: Counterpoint, 2013), 31.

2. Eugene H. Peterson, *Practice Resurrection: A Conversation on Growing Up in Christ* (Grand Rapids: Eerdmans, 2010), 8.

3. Robin Fasano, "How Prayer Changes Your Brain," *Spirituality and Health*, https://www.spiritualityhealth.com /how-prayer-changes-your-brain.

4. Andrew Newberg and Mark Robert Waldman, *How God Changes Your Brain: Breakthrough Findings from a Leading Neuroscientist* (New York: Ballantine, 2010).